ENDORSEMENTS

"There are as many paths to practice as there are the people who are serving as an end-of-life doula, and Melissa gives us a glimpse into hers. How beautiful and poignant, she speaks of how she accompanies people she loves and cares for through their death and beyond. The modalities Melissa uses and shares, her ways of caring, and her obvious passion will open your heart and mind."
Deanna Cochran, Founder, CareDoula® School of
Accompanying the Dying
Author of *Accompanying the Dying: Practical, Heart-Centered Wisdom for End-of-Life Doulas, and Health Care Advocates*

"*Persephone's Passage* provides readers with an in-depth glimpse into one woman's deeply personal journey toward one of the most complicated and empathetic professions of all time—a death doula. Melissa shares the intimate details of finding her way while facing the death of someone close to her—her own father."
Karen Hawkins, Author

"In a world too often reluctant to speak of death, this book is a gift. Melissa shares with beauty and grace her own journey with death, and that sharing offers each of us a hand to hold as we walk our own inevitable journeys, losing those we love. This book was especially timely for me, just a couple of weeks before I'll travel to spend time with a friend who is preparing for his own death. Thank you, Melissa."
Heather Plett, Author of
The Art of Holding Space: A Practice of Love, Liberation, and Leadership
Co-founder of the Centre for Holding Space

Persephone's Passage

Walking My Father into the Underworld
The Spiritual Journey of an End-of-Life Doula

Melissa Baker

Persephone's Passage:
Walking My Father into the Underworld
The Spiritual Journey of an End-of-Life Doula

Copyright © 2022 by Melissa Baker

ISBN: 978-1-7356932-8-6

ISBN: 1-7356932-8-6

Library of Congress Control Number: 2022903021

Cover Design by Thuan Nguyen, HouseOfThuan.com

Sacred Life Publishers™
SacredLife.com
Printed in the United States of America

About the Cover Art

This is a portion of an original painting by my SoulTribe Brother, H.B. Gardner. He once saw this image in a Felliniesque dream. Persephone crosses the River Styx on a barge, leaving her mother, Demeter to grieve. Hekate offers her torch to illuminate Her journey, and behind the Goddess of the Crossroads, Hermes, and Hades anticipate her arrival.

Dedicated to the beautiful, sacred souls of Lynn Thames, Bill Baker, and Brian Fawkes, beloved beings who inspired this journey and moved on without us, in that order. And to each of my fur-babies, who taught me about surrender, mercy, and deep grief, preparing me for my father's end-of-life journey. Their memories are a blessing.

This book is for those with the courage to sit down with Death and when fear and sorrow rise, offer Her welcome while holding space for the task of transformation that lies ahead.

CONTENTS

INTRODUCTION

In 2018, as I stepped out of my past life to create my future, crossroads merged. I was introduced to the emerging career path of an end-of-life doula, and my father's health began to decline.

This path of discovery, to determine what a post corporate life might hold for me, revealed itself to have been a greater gift than I could have imagined. Studying death and dying shifted my perspective and understanding of this natural part of life. It taught me how to find peace with the fact that we are all going to die, and that it is nothing to fear. Most significantly, it prepared me for the monumental loss of my father.

As I began my study, I dedicated this part of my life's journey to the archetype of Persephone. I chose Her because of her role as Goddess of the Underworld, yet she continues to reveal to me the depth and beauty of her mantle.

Persephone guides and supports sacred souls through their transition into the underworld, as they have departed the realm of the living. There, she is Queen. Yet, she is also the sacred daughter whose return delivers the coming of Spring. I feel blessed to be both of those things—daughter and guide.

As I now write, my father has been gone six months. Had he been a man too proud or too stubborn to allow his daughter to become his caregiver, I would have missed the greatest opportunity of my life. I am certain, at times, that he felt he was a burden to me. But I hope that he knew how his acts of surrender gave me the opportunity to learn and grow in service to his good care, and even more essential . . . he showed me the importance of allowing oneself to surrender and receive.

These pages started as homework and became my lifework. They captured enormous spiritual growth, emotional healing, and endless gratitude. My writing throughout this journey allowed friends and loved ones to follow along and, in some cases, to find their own peace and comfort with the mystery of what comes next.

You will find throughout this book that I spell magick with a "k". To me, magic means illusion while magick encompasses a moment made sacred. Magick is found in recognizing and following synchronicities that lead you into a joyful new beginning, or the way the wind blows through you and brings you to tears. Magick is found in moments of perfection when we are mindfully present with nature and those we love.

Since part of my book has been taken from numerous blog writings of mine, you will come across some repeats in the stories.

Thank you for walking this path with me. Whether you are on your own journey toward becoming Persephone or moving mindfully toward Persephone's Passage, I bid thee hail and welcome.

first evening shift available and I arrived to find my sweet and radiant friend lying in a darkened room, appearing small and depleted. She and I didn't speak at all during this visit; we had been informed that she preferred silence and rest at that point in time, and I spent my allotted time assisting her out of bed and to the bathroom and back into bed, and then sitting quietly at her feet, sending healing Reiki energy, while commanding her comfort until another devoted friend arrived for the next shift.

It was within the next week or two that I gleefully jumped ship from the toxic workplace and immediately reached out to Lynn's wife to inform her that I was now free to be present whenever I was needed. Despite transfusions, Lynn's blood count was not responding to treatment and she found comfort in having company in the hospital. So, I signed up for the next available morning shift and arrived at 10 a.m. To my delight, I found Lynn sitting up in bed talking to her friend and colleague. She glowed with recognition and introduced us, "This is Melissa . . . my dear friend of twenty-five years." When her colleague concluded her shift and passed the torch to me, I sat down for the important work of reconnecting.

If you asked me about my favorite place to be and my most fulfilling pastime, this would be it . . . sitting down in a comfortable space to deeply connect and share with loved ones the important details of our lives, with laughter and tears and absolute rapt attention. On this spectacular day, which will forever be one of my favorites, I was blessed to have eleven and a half hours doing just that with my beloved Lynn. I would quit that job a hundred times over for that blessing. I think, now, about how no one else had signed up for visitation that day, and how I felt completely free to just stay . . . and that I did just that. If someone else had arrived after four hours, I would have suffered such an unknown loss.

I joyfully recall the light that surrounded her as we talked and talked. Her white and red blood cells were both at zero, and yet, during our time together, she rested only fifteen or twenty minutes.

I don't know what delivered that energy for her, but I was so grateful to bear witness. We went right back to the beginning of our friendship—when we first met. It was a women's workshop at the Unitarian Church in Jacksonville that provided a momentous place in our shared history. Mom and I went together, and there we met up with our dear friends from our own church community, Ellen and Sharon. Their friend Marna also attended this event, and it was orchestrated for her to meet Lynn. When Lynn and Marna later found themselves free from committed relationships, they found a healthy and happy future in each other. Both were already on the healing path; Lynn, a mental health counselor, and Marna, a massage therapist with an interest in Native American spirituality, and together they grew into healers through Chinese Medicine with a continued passion for teaching and bringing improved health to others.

Life had gotten in the way, and we hadn't seen much of each other over the last several years, though we wouldn't miss an opportunity when presented. I remember gathering at their home in 2009, where we manifested a dream that I'd had a year or two before. When our friend, Sharon, was going through treatment for cervical cancer, the prayer or—better, the belief—that I sent into the Universe was that Sharon would get through this difficult time, and we sisters would once again gather around the fire circle, raising our voices in song while she played dulcimer and Lynn played guitar. That night I cried tears of joy. This was just one of the stories I shared with Lynn on that magickal day we shared. I reminded her of how nearly twenty-five years ago, as we discussed in a group studying Harville Hendrix's *Getting the Love You Want*, it was she who alerted me to the understanding of my childhood memories of being bullied. She pointed out that because my brother was seven years older than me, and our relationship was not combative, I never learned to defend myself, which made me an easy target.

leaf falls to the ground, transforming into rich fertile earth that will feed the roots of the tree from which they've fallen.

Throughout our lives, we come to our own autumn season—when it is time to reflect on the beauty and the darkness of what has gone before, to honor those moments and lessons, to give thanks—even for the darkness (for it has shown us the light)—to let them gently fall away, and to prepare for what is yet to come.

Remember that once the leaves fall from the tree of life, there is a period of rest followed by the surprising *pop* of new growth, so vibrant and stunning, a stark contrast from the nakedness of dormancy that we cannot help but celebrate the utter joy of new life being presented.

So, here's to the coming of autumn; to the beauty, to the sorrow, to the gratitude, to the slumber, to the waking, and to the rebirth. Gather it into a great big cushy pile and fall back into it. Bury yourself in the memories and—finally—emerge with a smile, brush yourself off, and move forward into the light.

There were other signposts along my journey of self-discovery as well. In January of 2018, a friend was diagnosed with colon cancer and would begin a journey of healing and recovery. I count this experience in my ability to serve and to lead, as the part I played was to become her communications director. I created and initiated her Caring Bridge page, and until she had the strength and fortitude to connect on her own, I followed her progress closely and skillfully shared upbeat updates (as she would have it) with friends and family. I continue to sit firmly among Team Jules, being of service wherever needed. She has a great team, and we take turns assisting her with chemo appointments, cat care (no litter box scooping for her throughout chemo), etc. Here's an example of one of the post-op updates.

And So, It Begins . . .
Journal entry by Melissa Baker – Feb 20, 2018

When it was suggested that I start a blog, this was not really what I'd dreamed it might be but there is no better cause I can imagine supporting, and since I know she doesn't want me to cook for her—I have offered my words:

> Hi there! My name is Melissa, and I'll be Julie's cruise director. In the days ahead, I will be sharing with all of you important news on surgical success and progress reports. I hear that passing gas is big news in the world that follows colon surgery.
>
> We all want to know how to help our beloveds during challenging moments in life, and I promise that we will all have opportunities to be her torch bearers. There may soon be a schedule for hospital sitting, food delivery, cat litter scooping—the possibilities are endless!
>
> Know that we are enormously grateful for your compassion, for your empathy, for your loving kindness, and for your devotion. We believe in the very best possible outcome, and with your shared focus, positive energy, and pure light from within . . . we will get there with grace and ease.

And then, there was the opportunity to serve Ellen and Sharon (mentioned in my story about Lynn). They are two of my most honored and sacred crones, each with health issues that needed addressing in the first half of that year. I became their driver, their wheelchair maiden, and their personal assistant—texting Sharon with reminders of medical guidance from doctor and pharmacist so that we'd both have it in writing—and keeping Ellen's daughter updated on situations when she could not be present. Truly, this sabbatical from the workplace had given me the opportunity to be of service to those I love, without limitation or regret.

But the relationship that I initially mentioned is where it first occurred to me that I might be called not to be a life coach, but an end-of-life coach. I met Brian through my brief association with the workplace I left before Lynn died. We met on my first day with the company, and it was love at first sight. We resonated with one another from the get-go, probably a past life thing. He worked remotely, but would come into town on occasion for on-site work. In February 2018, we had a dinner date to catch up on each other's lives since I left the company. This was when he so courageously shared with me the prognosis of a diagnosis he'd been dealing with for some time before we met. The prostate cancer was in his bones. At the time, he was on experimental treatment that he ultimately hoped would prolong life, knowing that it could not save it. I later learned that the treatment nearly killed him.

Somehow, I found words for him, "Brian, you have been given a deadline. What is your joy?"

He looked at me and said, "Melissa, no one has ever asked me that before." I had a list of other questions or suggestions for him, as well, that we discussed over dinner, and later typed up in an email for his reflection; for discussion on his next business trip into town.

We kept in touch through email and text messaging between visits. One of his messages to me informed me of his joy. "It's Derek," he said. His husband is his joy. Over dinner on his next visit, he spoke of his husband of more than two decades who dotes on him and worries about him through complications of his illness. He started to share how terrible it feels to know that Derek is losing sleep for his care . . . and how Brian wished he wouldn't. I looked into the eyes of my new friend and I demanded that he allow his husband to do absolutely everything for him that he chooses, reminding Brian that when this sweet man's beloved is no longer upon the earth he will never have to question if he had done enough for his love and comfort. We also discussed protection of resources, like whether the house was in both of their names, and if he could research the possibility of cashing in his 401K with a penalty since he might not be here at age sixty-five. Shouldn't he be able to use it to make earthly dreams come true before he leaves his body behind? At the time, I didn't know if that was possible (I learned so much in the months that followed), but you know . . . it was a pretty good question, right? Another suggestion I made, when I learned that his husband loves the task of renovating a house that he owns in California, was about his work situation. He only goes to work on that project when Brian is away for business.

I inquired, "Since you can work from anywhere, Brian, why don't you go with him? You can sit in the healing California sun while Derek works on his passion project." I was thrilled to learn, in a later message, from my soul friend that, until I mentioned it over lunch on his last visit, it had never occurred to him and that starting that month, he was going to work from their home in California.

We continued to share occasional love notes via text. I remind him that I am holding him close and that I hope he is filling each moment with joy, and he reminds me that I have made a difference in his life. Aside from the miraculous and complete, spontaneous healing of this sacred soul—nothing could make me happier than to know this. He truly holds a piece of my heart, and I believe that *he* is the most significant catalyst for my current quest.

Thanks to these beautiful beings in my life, allowing me the opportunity to be of service, I trusted the direction where I felt led. I reached out to Deanna Cochran to purchase her self-paced home study course for becoming an end-of-life doula. It was before the term was widely known (at least in my social circle), and at the point just before she gave birth to an official certification school and her own book on providing care at the end of life. If you feel led, as I did, I highly recommend that you consider seeking her guidance and counsel through the CareDoula® School for Accompanying the Dying. Her book is called *Accompanying the Dying: Practical, Heart-Centered Wisdom for End-of-Life Doulas and Healthcare Advocates.*

THE HOMEWORK

Stepping onto this path in early 2018, I embarked on the homework assigned by Deanna Cochran for her End-of-Life Doula self-study course. At the time, my experience with death was, gratefully, limited. This section of writing was from that moment in time. This reflection played a role in the years that followed as I consciously cared for my father, intending not to fail him. Having identified the encounters I had with death before educating myself, I was clear on what I would do differently while serving my parents.

This process gave me the opportunity to reflect on my strengths and limitations over the years. It certainly brought to the surface a few regrets and feelings of shame, which deserved my attention. In taking the time to walk through these stories of loss, I was able to hold space for my former self. While sitting with my younger self in those historic spaces, I offered her empathy and forgiveness.

Later that year, I started a blog, and stopped focusing on writing in my homework journal, and started sharing what I was learning in a more open space. This book combines what I have learned from formal study, and what I learned through mindful living as I cared for my father through the last years of his life. May it be a blessing to others.

MY EXPERIENCE WITH DEATH AND DYING

As my soul is feeling called in the direction of end-of-life doula, I reflect on my personal experience with death as is instructed in the course materials. Now surrounded by books on death and dying—reading the beautiful, heartbreaking, healing, inspiring, uplifting stories of the gentle passing of souls—I investigate my own life of loss and realize that I am blessed to have lost so few beloveds in the last forty-nine years.

My first great loss was my maternal grandmother. I was only in elementary school when she slipped through the veil and, though she had suffered strokes before her death, I can recall sitting with her and holding her elevated hand in the hospital bed granddaddy had brought into the room which is now my library. If I were to turn to look behind me now, she would be there.

My memories of Nanny are all sweet and warm. Sitting in bed with her in the room, which is now my bedroom, the 1950s windows cranked open, walls painted green, shelves holding pictures of her beloved family . . . her only living child, my mother, with husband and a boy and a girl, and the son she had lost in his mid-thirties to a blood clot after abdominal surgery . . . such a beautiful face, that I would only know through photos.

In the kitchen, beneath scalloped window frame, I stood on a chair to help wash the dishes. My brother, John, and I would step out the kitchen door to eat tomatoes like apples with a shake of salt. I would sit at the secretary desk, where she had placed a chair, pulled out the drawer, and released the drawbridge-like writing surface for my "drawing" pleasure. There was a light-blue plastic

Dutch-style shoe that contained pencils and, with zero artistic ability, I would sit and scribble, feeling like a gifted artist with her loving presence and acknowledgment.

We don't have an awareness of time through her illness and passing. How long was she in that bed after her stroke? When exactly did she die? I think it was in 1977 . . . at least that was what I recall from the headstone I eventually found in Greenwood Cemetery, somewhere in my mid-twenties. There was no real goodbye . . . I came home from school one day and the bottle of polish that she used to paint her toenails, a shade of brightest red was sitting in the chair by the front door. I asked Mom why it was there and I learned she was gone.

There was no funeral service, no memorial. She was buried without our witness and we never visited her grave. I've been living in her house for the past twenty years, and friends with intuitive and medium gifts have confirmed her presence, warm and loving energy. I am no medium, but I love knowing that she is here—an energy signature in the molecules of this sacred space, which surround me and are eternally within me. A friend once said that walking into my house was like walking into a hug. Now, I wonder if that is Nanny greeting each of my friends as they enter to show her gratitude for their presence in the life of her only granddaughter.

The next great loss for our family was my Aunt Beth. It was she who introduced my parents, long ago. Beth and my mom worked together at the phone company and she brought Mom home to her large family for dinner. My dad is one of seven kids, and I can only imagine what entering that family must have been like for virtually an only child. Mom's brother, Jimmy, was twenty years old when he was in the Navy and introduced her parents to one another. When he died, Mom was only sixteen and had lost her favorite pen pal, who wrote to her of penguins on the ship as they passed through the Antarctic region on a tour of duty. And so, it must have been quite a culture shock to be suddenly surrounded by so much family when one's family had previously been so small.

When she was forty, my Aunt Beth was diagnosed with ovarian cancer. I remember seeing her in the hospital after she had her hysterectomy, and I saw her at the Red Log House where my grandparents lived until it was time to simplify their lives due to aging. She went through chemotherapy; the cancer won and we all lost. I was in the fourth grade. My memories of this time are few, but I recall that this was one of two times in my life I would see my dad cry. I remember being in Mrs. Pereda's classroom one day and lingering behind as the rest of my class exited for recess or lunch. The presence of warmth, compassion, and understanding came through our custodian, Mrs. Castaneda, who hugged me as I cried. Only vaguely do I recall attending Beth's funeral. I still wonder how different life would have been for her boys had they not lost their mother at such a tender age, both in middle school.

Next in my line of loss, ten years after Nanny died, Granddaddy was stricken with a brain tumor, which quickly rendered him no longer independent, and memory deficient. I was fifteen. I can recall the hurt that I felt when he addressed my presence, asking if I worked at the hospital . . . oblivious to my status as his only granddaughter. I think the accurate emotion may have been fear. I regret that I was not evolved enough at that age, to be a better participant in his departure and of greater support to my mom in her grief. My final memory was feeding him careful bites of Mom's home-cooked meal as he stared ahead, lacking language and connectedness. Fifteen was a difficult year, and I was already cried out with my own first-love heartbreak when Mom gave me the news of his passing one morning.

Again, there was no funeral and no memorial. One day, granddaddy took residence in our hall closet. Later that year we took a cruise to Mexico to release his ashes into the sea. He had been a career US Navy chief machinist. With a ship filled with high school seniors—intoxicated and scattered about the entire vessel—my mom and dad eventually slipped out of our cabin at 3 a.m. to let his ashes go gently into the wind and water. Again, I wish I had been a different version of myself at that time. Looking back, I was probably dealing with depression. I slept much of the time we were on board. I wish I had been there with my mother rather than asleep in our cabin. I wish I knew then what I know now about the importance of words and ceremony. I wish that I could have been capable of bringing her comfort and peace for a relationship that was more complicated than I understood at that age.

When Freddie Mercury died, I was twenty-three. His loss inspired me to volunteer with a local organization that supported people living with HIV. I became a "buddy" in the buddy program, and was introduced to Kirby in January. He was a beautiful soul. His parents cared for him in their home, and I would come by to sit with him so they could go to church together and have a moment of comfort amid sorrow. Kirby was bedridden when I met him, but he was still able to communicate. One of the first things he said to me when his parents left was, "Melissa, I am being punished because I strayed from God." This just broke my heart. I am not Christian, and the idea that a person of faith could feel so lost due to illness felt horrifying to me. He was the choir director at his gospel church, and had a blood transfusion in the mid-eighties, after his appendix ruptured. I visited with him a few times when his mother invited my company . . . and together we would laugh and watch videos of his favorite gospel choir. My final memories of Kirby were in the hospital. Once I saw him right after he got his braces off and I could read in his eyes that he recognized me, though he no longer had the strength to push out breath for speech. I remember feeling inadequate with my words, and not knowing what to say. I just wanted to wrap him in my love. I hope he could feel that and I believe that he did. The last time I saw him was in his hospital bed, surrounded by family and friends. Though I was the only non-Christian white girl in the room, they welcomed me into their circle and we all prayed together for his peaceful passing.

Kirby died a week before his twenty-eighth birthday. I attended his wake at 910, a local gospel church where he used to sing and direct the choir on Sundays. The music was beautiful and moving and I was compelled to stand and sway, and I laughed with tears in my eyes as I realized that I was not capable of clapping on the offbeat. I knew that Kirby was laughing with me. I kept in touch with his mom for a long time after his departure. She would always remind me that I was the first person she ever left her baby alone with during his long illness. In fact, I just called her today and she said it again. It was my great honor to know and to serve Kirby from January through October of my twenty-fourth year . . . but I was not emotionally able, at that age, to put myself out there again. Kirby was my one and only buddy. I will never forget the way that his light filled the room.

Also, when I was twenty-three, my mom signed me up for a six-month class on Wicca. She knew I was curious after learning of the rumored spiritual path of a certain rock and roll songstress. One of the teachers was called Ken Windwalker. He was open about his HIV status and had taken good care of himself, made his own kombucha tea, and took other healing supplements. Five years after our class, Ken developed a kind of leukemia that was typical of the side door illnesses that could come with HIV positive diagnoses. We gathered to see him in the hospital, and with a very quick decline, we gathered in his home to sit vigil. I remember sitting by his bed and singing to him. He loved to sing and that was one of the gifts he offered from our class, which was to chant in celebration of the Goddess, the elements, the seasons of life, and earth. I sang to my teacher the healing chant that I learned at my first healing circle, which affirmed my place on this spiritual path back in 1992, "I am a circle; I am healing you. You are a circle; you are healing me. Unite us, be one. Unite us, be as one."

The next day, we received the call from his husband that he had passed into the Summerland, which is the Heaven equivalent on the Wiccan path. This time, I was evolved enough to handle this departure with grace and purpose. I partnered with his husband to create a memorial service that would bring comfort to those who loved Windwalker, both Pagans and Christians. I engaged the Pagan choir and I ran between lectern and choir stand to speak, to introduce, and to sing, accordingly, throughout the event.

Though we were only twenty-eight, the fact that Windwalker died at the young age of thirty-two, my partner (at the time) and I were inspired. We had our first wills and end-of-life care plans written up that year. Windwalker had refused, even through his illness to discuss these things with his life-partner and I witnessed the turmoil it created. The one who loved him so deeply, worried he might not handle things as his lost love would have wished. He questioned every little decision rather than having the comfort of knowing for sure that his actions would be right and true.

With the loss of my friend and teacher, I have two regrets that shifted the way I moved through the world when he was gone. They were both missed opportunities. One was an invitation to work one-on-one with him to deepen my meditation practice, and the second was an anniversary dinner that was missed due to weather and feeling grumpy. When he was gone, so were those opportunities to gather, to celebrate, to learn, and grow with his guidance and support. I would never again take such opportunities with others for granted. I always consider that the invitation may not come again.

My paternal grandfather's departure came many years after we lost his eldest daughter. Bumpa was diagnosed with leukemia in his early eighties and, long into that decade, he grew tired of taking the pills of poison each day and decided he was ready to go. He said that he asked his doctor how long it would take for him to die once he quit taking the chemo and consuming food, and then chose to go. So, we gathered as a family in my grandparents' home, which we had not done often in their later years. There were DNR (do not resuscitate) signs throughout the house, to ensure that if a medical worker entered as he was dying he would not be brought back against his will. The family respected and honored his wishes, and we all had the chance to say goodbye.

As I prepared to depart for a mountain vacation the following week, I asked Bumpa if he felt I should stay. He insisted I go, and a few days into it I made the call (before cell phones) to learn that he was gone. Since I was not able to attend his funeral, I chose to create my own private ritual. The cabin where we were staying had a wood burning stove in the living room. I sat down with paper and pen and wrote him a letter. I filled it with words of love, gratitude, and sweet memories. I kissed it, folded it, and placed it into the stove, asking the smoke of fire and air to deliver my words to his soul.

When he was gone, I would visit with Nana and ask how she was doing. Her reply was always, "I'm just waiting." And wait, she did. It was fourteen years of life without Bumpa before she finally declined. That was after knitting dozens of blankets and hundreds of scarves. My Auntie M, her youngest daughter, was her primary caregiver since Bumpa died. Sadly, as she was preparing for the loss of her mother, she was also caring for her husband who was dying of lung cancer. Uncle G's insistence that his condition be kept within their nuclear family meant that most of us were unaware of his suffering. We could not ease the burden that his wife and daughters carried.

They did have home hospice assistance, but policy prevented them from giving him the level of pain management that he needed. So, he finally allowed the move to a hospice facility and very quickly received the peace he deserved. It was as if his suffering was holding him in this life and when the pain could be managed, his body could relax and release his soul.

I don't know if it was pride, stubbornness, or disbelief that required this secret be kept. I do suspect it complicated his end-of-life journey. I know it was hard for all involved. It was through the stories that my aunt shared with me that I found myself advising others, recently. Because my uncle didn't want work to know that he was terminal, my aunt lost benefits. He could have retired before going out on leave, and the difference in surviving spouse benefits would have greatly served his wife, now widow, of thirty-three years.

After Uncle G found peace, Nana slowed down and stopped getting out of bed. She was ninety-nine. When it was no longer possible to care for her at home, she went to hospice where her six remaining children took turns sitting with her. She had pretty much gone to sleep, until she finally slipped through the veil as my uncle slept in the chair by her bed. I was grateful for the many years that I had chosen to visit with her whenever I could. She would tell me many of the same stories each time I visited. I always received them with a smile and sheer enjoyment as if each time brought a new tale. When she died, I sat down to write about my memories of her, and this is what I shared with my family on the day of her memorial. It was, for me, as if I had been given the gift to go back in time. And these words just poured onto the page.

Remembering Nana

If you asked me what I did last weekend, I would have to refer to my calendar to find an ounce of recall to share with you how I filled my days. There are movies I've watched and books I've read that must be watched again and reread, for I cannot recall the names of characters or how the story ends. But the many family gatherings of my childhood seem to be woven into my being, like the yarn that Nana wove into blankets, toilet roll covers, tree skirts, caps for newborns, and scarves for really, *really* tall people.

These last few days, I have found myself wandering through an old familiar place. I see it in my mind like a 1970s color photograph that is awash in warm sunlight. To me, it was—and remains—the most magical place I know. If we could still walk through that mystical Log House on Seminola, we would come down that inviting circular driveway and the sweet gardenias and roses would assault our senses. Looking out to the side yard near the road, we would see the egg carton flowers on the prickly bush, and we would know that Nana was nearby.

The front door is always open, so we pull open the screen door with a *squeeeeak* and let it slam behind us as we enter. The brass pipes of the clock that never seemed to work are to the left, and we stop to make it chime by flicking each note with a fingernail. Further to the left is the doorway and pass through to the kitchen— and there's Bumpa, with a big voice and a toothy grin greeting us with a kiss and a snack. Nana is at the piano . . . still practicing. Suddenly, the house is filled with the warmth of familiar voices. All the Baker kids are here with their young families: Billy and Bethy, Richard and Kenny, Patty, Mikey, and Marianne. I know we weren't all small at the same time, but it is a magical house and so the blood descendants of Bill and Lil are found running through the living room, down the steps, into the family room with the Lake Tahoe Mural on the right wall and the secret bedroom to the left, toward the picture window that frames the sacred oak trees and Lake Katherine, out the door to the right, and jumping into the pool. There are Johnny and Chad, Jeremy and Missy, Dari, Chris, Jonah, Kelly, Carrie, and Erin. The sun is shining and there are bushels of honeysuckle blossoms along the fence to be plucked and drained of their sweet nectar. To me, this is heaven. This is where I want to go when I die. Back to the bosom of my family in a time filled with youth and optimism.

That's not to say that I would trade the life I've lived since that time, for when our grandparents were slowing down and hosting less; the years that followed the departure from the Log House offered the quiet time, when I had grown more mature and could sit quietly with Nana to learn how to crochet while Bumpa napped in his den, and I could truly appreciate the stories she would share about the life she had lived. There were stories that predated this family dream . . . about her mother and sister, and Mr. McCarthy; about explaining to the Nuns that she had to leave school to go to work with her mother as a seamstress making awnings, and working for Baker's Chocolate before she ever fell in love with a man named Baker; about floating in the waters of the Quincy Bay where she met the Baker Girls that led to meeting Bumpa; about how she had ten bridesmaids who planned her entire wedding, including selecting the dress. And my favorite story of all is how when her mother died, her phone rang . . . and she heard her mother's voice calling, "Lily!"

This flood of memory is not just about Nana or Lovely Lily, as my immortal grandmother shall become in my mind—it is about the sacred family that she and Bumpa created together and how despite our years of separation by life and geography, each and every one of you have continued to live with me every day, inside my heart, within a magical red log house . . . and this sacred space is where we can still go to see those we have lost. Our Beautiful Beth, Our Beloved Bumpa, Our Gregarious Gregg, and our Lovely Lily. Please join me in a moment of prayer.

> Hail to thee, beloved mother, sacred grand-mother, Lovely Lily of the moonlit hair . . . we stand before you with gratitude and reverence for ninety-nine years upon the earth, for seventy-three years of motherhood, for forty-nine years of grandmother-hood, and for overwhelming us with love and

nurturing throughout these many years. Thank you for tiny, grey, hand-stitched mice dressed in tuxedos and tutus. Thank you for homemade eggnog and magic bars of chocolate and coconut. Thank you for every story you shared that allowed us to know you as more than a mother or grandmother. Thank you for *every single* stitch in *every single* afghan that you knitted or crocheted for each of us, every year. If ever we feel that you are too far away, all we will need to do is wrap ourselves in a Nana blanket and we shall feel cloaked within your eternal love. Blessed be. Nana, just so you know . . . I'll be waiting by the phone.

Wanting to Serve

A few years ago, I was introduced to a woman in my social circle named Rebecca. I didn't have the opportunity to know her well. She had been diagnosed with ovarian cancer and simply wasn't well enough to join us often. Though she had gone through surgery and treatment, her CA125 numbers continued to rise. She was a therapist who brought comfort to many, but it felt as if she was struggling to find comfort for herself. I offered support in those brief conversations, but really didn't know how to provide useful care. When she went into hospice, the best I could do for someone I barely knew—who had not asked for my presence or support— was to bring food. At the time, I worked for a restaurant company with multiple brands. So, over the course of several weeks I would pick up food after work and deliver it to the hospice. For a while, she enjoyed the decadence of my deliveries, but the last time I saw her I was informed that her organs had begun to shut down and that her body really couldn't do anything with the intake. What I delivered ended up being more for the family and staff . . . which was fine. I realize now that what she really needed was company. At the time, I felt awkward about that because she didn't really know me. I couldn't imagine that a dying person would find comfort with a stranger, but I see that differently now. I wish I better understood at the time, how to serve her well. She died within a week of my last delivery of sustenance that she could not consume. I was so ignorant about death at the time. I realize that my presence brings comfort. I am a gifted listener—free of judgment, which allows others to feel safe speaking their truth. If I could go back, I would sit with Rebecca and ask her about her dreams and regrets. I would seek the stories she wanted to share and celebrate with her the many gifts she delivered to the world. I would hope to comfort her fears.

May I be forgiven for what I did not yet understand. May I be redeemed in the future by showing up, and by holding space for and through discomfort. May I be brave enough not to run from death. If invited, may my presence be a comfort to each courageous being at the occasion of their grand departure.

PATTERNS OF AWARENESS

I'm not sure about patterns in these losses, but I do see an evolution of capability. As I've aged, I have learned how to be present for those who need to be heard. I am skilled at being of service and supportive when others are grieving. I once had no words, and now I understand that words are not always needed; presence and compassion are far more important. Holding space for others to mourn and to heal is important. Planning for the end-of-life is important, and it is the most compassionate thing we can do for our loved ones. A discussion long before a diagnosis can be had in the absence of grief and fear. It is a part of the comfort one may find upon departure, to know that they are leaving their beloveds simply to grieve.

GOING DEEP

Another question asked is about comfort in receiving emotional support, such as a hug, from strangers. At first, I couldn't think of an instance, until I realized that I had only written about the humans that I have lost and not about my beloved pets. In my adult and independent life—in other words, since I moved out of my parents' home—I have loved, nurtured, and cared for cats. Of five fur-babies that have blessed my life (as of early 2018), I have lost four. Each loss was devastating. When I compare these losses to my human ones, I recognize that the suffering at each loss was extensive. I imagine the reason is multi-tiered and multi-teared.

First, I was completely responsible for their care and well-being. If they suffered, it was because of my neglect or inability to understand their needs. If only they could speak or I could understand their language. That leaves a world of opportunity for self-flagellation. Secondly, unlike the people I have lost, my pets have been with me every single day through prosperity and hardship, anywhere from two-to-nineteen years. Finally, unlike most relationships in life, they loved me without condition and they each played an important role in nurturing my identity and, at times, my self-worth.

The day that came forward in my memory, with the question of how I feel about receiving comfort from strangers, was a few years back when Nightshade died. She had been with me for nineteen years and she was a cat that only a mother could love. She looked so inviting to pet, but then she would often snap and growl if you tried. She would follow my friends into the bathroom then hiss at them when she realized they were not me. She also had a

this moment, I would designate both of my parents and my brother. This may change should my future include a partner, or I may ask this of a very close friend should I outlive my family.

The second *wish* is for the kind of medical treatment I want or don't want. This is where I inform my caregiver that I do not want to be in pain. I wish to be medicated to relieve my pain, even if it leads to more sleep. I want to be kept warm, clean, and dry at all times. If I am near death, I do not wish to be fed or watered, as I see that to be an act of prolonging my suffering.

The form goes into great detail about the meaning of "life support treatment" and allows for making adjustments to accommodate personal or religious beliefs. If Death with Dignity for a compassionate end is available where I live, I would like to have it administered with any terminal diagnosis. If I am close to death, in a coma without hope of full recovery, have suffered severe brain damage, or have been diagnosed with severe dementia—unable to recognize myself or others—I do not want life-support treatment. If it has been started, I want it stopped. I wish to die with dignity and have my soul liberated from the confines of this body when there is no quality of life remaining.

The third *wish* is for how comfortable I want to be. What a great prompt this is. I wonder if any of us would give this a thought otherwise. There are multiple choices and those that don't apply are simply crossed through. This really makes me think about how I'd like to be treated now and always, not just when I'm dying. I love that this offers instruction for the designated caregiver. Otherwise, this moment might be too overwhelming and emotional to consider the possibilities. Again, I don't want to be in pain and would like to be medicated. If I appear sad or ill, I want my caregivers to do what they can to help make me feel better. Should I have a fever, I'd like to be gently cooled. I would like my lips and mouth to be kept moist. I wish to be kept clean, warm, and dry. I wish to have my favorite music playing until my time of death. I would love for someone to read to me either something they've written, poetry, or from one of my favorite books (maybe this one). When the time comes, I wish to engage hospice care to nurture me and my loved ones.

The fourth *wish* is how I want people to treat me. Again, why wait? I would love to have people with me when possible, including my family, my tribe, and my life-long friends. I don't fear dying alone, but I do love the idea of sweet witness and companionship at the end. I want to have my hands held and stories told, even if it seems I cannot respond. I wish to have the good wishes, the healing energy, and the prayers for peace of all who know me, in whatever form feels true to them. I would be honored if someone would say the phowa for me if I cannot follow the practice myself. I always want to be cared for with kindness and compassion. I won't ask you not to be sad or expect you to be cheerful. I mean, I sincerely hope that you will miss me when I'm gone. Because I know that is how I will feel should you go first. But a joyful, grateful, peaceful presence will always be welcome—dying or not. Dying at home sounds ideal, especially if I get to die in my sleep, but I won't say not to take me to a hospice or hospital. I want my death to be a peaceful transition for myself and those who care for me. I understand that home may not provide that. Let's play that part by ear, shall we?

The fifth *wish* is what I want my loved ones to know. Oh, goodness. There are lots of prompts provided, but I have a feeling I can come up with my own. Once again, I feel these are things that should be spoken often, not just near death. For this, I'm just going to be direct. I want you to know that being your daughter, sister, niece, cousin, grandaunt, faery goddess mother, a life-long friend has been the greatest blessing of my life. If there is anything I did to cause you harm that has not yet been addressed, I hope that you will forgive me now. I hold no grudges and have nothing in my heart left to forgive. If you are worried there might be something, know that you are forgiven. I want you to understand that though I will miss your warm embrace, I eagerly walk toward the veil of transformation and look forward to returning to the light of truth. In that light of oneness, know that I will always be with you. May you know for all of your days, that I still love you most.

My dreams for loved ones that I shall leave behind are that they find a way to be mindful and present for the rest of their days. That their dreams no longer lie dormant in the recesses of their minds but are made manifest with the knowledge that time upon the earth is limited and precious . . . it is of absolute priority to take full advantage of each day. I hope that they will remember me well, but not dwell on my absence. I will be right there beside each of them when my body is no longer a burden, and my spirit has been set free. All they will ever have to do is hold their left hand out with their palm facing upward, and there I shall rest the energetic essence of my abiding love for each of them.

In my sacred space of leaving, I would enjoy candlelight with myrrh incense burning nearby. Music playing quietly, probably in the realm of relaxing Celtic instrumental. Maybe I'll create a playlist. Gentle massage would be welcome, though I am normally a fan of deep tissue, just something soothing that makes my tired body feel valued and loved the way it has always deserved. Besides my family and partner, should I have acquired one by then, I would request the presence of a few key people, either for a moment or through to the end; my lifelong friends, my tribe, my soul sisters and brothers. I have a list with phone numbers.

Now, a few specifics for what comes next. If any part of my body may be used to benefit the life of another, I gladly give it. I am a registered organ donor. I wish for whatever remains of my body to be cremated. I have learned that the pre-paid cremation plans cost double what it would cost to simply call a local crematorium when the time comes. I will have the funds available to cover the expense. Don't waste money on the funeral home. My celebration will not be held in a space like that. If it is available, I would prefer water cremation over the higher environmental impact caused by fire. At this time, there is no specific place I'd like to have my remains scattered. Perhaps someday there will be someone in my life who cares about that. If not, plant me with an oak tree or scatter me on the Blue Ridge Parkway at the base of a waterfall. I promise, my consciousness will be free from attachment to outcome.

When I think about my own end of life and what type of service I would have, I realize that I would hate to miss the party. So, instead of a memorial service when I am gone, I would rather have a living wake while I am still here . . . that is to say, if I have a terminal illness and have been given a relative timeline for departure. So, if I were not to die—unexpectedly in my sleep, or falling off a cliff in Ireland—I would command a celebration! It would be a veritable love fest allowing me the chance to inform dear ones of their importance in this world and in my life.

At this celebration, there would be plenty of comfortable seating, like a large living room, where everyone can put their feet up and cuddle on the couch. There would be comfort food and dark chocolate, and lots of time to connect with each loved one in attendance. We would discuss our first memories of one another, and share meaningful stories that affirm our friendship and gratitude for this life we've been blessed to enjoy together. There may need to be a timekeeper to ensure everyone has time to connect. There would be music playing at a volume that allows conversation. To include, but not be limited to: Stevie Nicks, Fleetwood Mac, Lisa Thiel, KIVA, Queen, Bee Gees, Loreena McKennitt, Clannad, VAS, to name a few.

I'm unattached to the idea of a Memorial Service, for I feel that is for the living and I will no longer be in human form. However, if I were to plan something for my loved ones to share in my absence, it would probably be in ritual format, with an invitation to the elements and to my beloved goddesses, Artemis and Persephone

gratitude. For the love that you have offered so freely, not only to me but to your family, your friends, your community, our planet, and all Her beloved creatures . . . I love you more."

SERVING BEFORE THE FINAL PHASE

Understanding that we may be of service before the dying phase has begun, the services that resonate with me and work with my strengths would be companion and comforter, patient advocate, letter/story recorder, walking through decisions that might feel too overwhelming, helping one to find clarity through the fog of fear and sorrow. I have acted as patient advocate in my personal life, with parents and friends who may not think to ask certain questions, or whose loved ones cannot be present for an important appointment. I record the meeting with the doctor, so that instructions are not forgotten in the chaos of hospital mechanics. This is especially helpful in eldercare, as we seem to live more in the now as we age — holding onto less of what we may have heard yesterday. Since being of service is my joy, I imagine that whatever is required, I will somehow become.

ENCOURAGING HOSPICE

When we talk about the suffering of a loved one in the disease process, the first memory is of my Uncle G, though I am only aware of stories, as he refused to allow his family to share his status of frailty. My aunt and cousins witnessed his suffering daily, which came along with his bad moods due to pain. (We all know that being in pain causes us to feel grouchy and on edge.) My outsider's opinion assumes he felt that hospice would be the path for a weaker man. But these many years later, I'm still bitter about what my aunt had to endure. I regret his ignorance, for it caused undue hardship for those who loved him. More than that, I regret that he suffered so greatly. His ailment was lung cancer, and I've heard that to be excruciating. My aunt was so relieved when he relented. He could finally rest when he arrived at hospice, and he let go of his body within a few days. If any of us who were not within his inner circle had been aware, there might have been a mindful plea for his comfort and a choice to spare his children and wife the torture of his suffering.

Through my study of palliative care and hospice, I feel that the main adjustment in my understanding and possible advice is that when there is not a quality of life that will allow the achievement of dreams, comfort should be key. On a personal note, I feel that I would limit my own life-prolonging tactics once I have lost the possibility of feeling well enough to enjoy life with my loved ones. If I can't stay mindful and present while being free from pain, I don't feel that I would want to continue eating when I am not hungry, etc. I would choose not to prolong my death, were there no more living to be had.

This is where my homework ends, and my blog begins. I've pulled the pages from that platform into this book, because they are an offering of my journey as it occurred. I have what I call a Swiss cheese memory, where important details tend to fall through the holes. Maintaining a blog provided a safe space for my thoughts and experiences in relative real time before too much was lost.

These pages contain the progression of a story shared with my father, which turned out to be the last three-and-a-half years of his life. As I reread these posts, I was so grateful for my mindfulness to write it all down. There were already important details I'd forgotten and I was so glad to have handed those memories back to myself.

THE JOURNEY

Entries from Bee the Light
Sacred Ceremony – June 2018

I was first introduced to sacred ceremony in 1992 at a workshop on feminine spirituality. In my circle it is also referred to as "ritual," but since those unfamiliar with the practice may have only heard the term followed with the word "sacrifice," I prefer the above. Sacred ceremonies you may be familiar with would be a child's christening or a wedding. If you consider how important these rites of passage are for the child, the couple, and their community, understand that there are many moments in our lives that deserve to be marked and celebrated and that the act of doing so will make the milestone or accomplishment more sacred. At times, there are obstacles to overcome like a great loss, heartbreak, or regrets that get in the way of our own progress. This is when I find the art of ceremony to be most rewarding and deeply healing.

We lost a beloved member of our community to leukemia in November. In December, a conversation with her widow revealed that she wasn't sleeping well, and that she was having trouble dealing with emotions of anger and bitterness toward an organization that had mistreated Lynn a few years before her death. The betrayal she suffered led her into a spiral of depression and a crisis of identity from which she never really recovered. I assured my friend that her love left behind all of those worries with her body and that she carried them no longer, which is what she surely would wish for those who survived her. I offered suggestions for cutting off from that energy and asked her to let me know if she needed support in doing so. At our next check-in she affirmed her desire for help in letting go.

So, we came together at the dark of moon. Lakeside and surrounding a brilliant bowl of fire, we set an altar of our reverence. There was a large, framed photo of Lynn's beautiful smiling face, radiant with sunshine. There were also a few sacred symbols and her guitar, with which she had formerly serenaded us all at campfires past. With the couple who had eagerly introduced our beloved to her wife a quarter century before, and another couple from their shared inner circle, we gathered. This was not a memorial for we had done that exceptionally well in the fall. This was an intentional ceremony of release for those who remained to face life without the presence of a sacred soul held dear.

These were the words that stated our purpose and intention for this ceremony:

> We gather to reconnect this sacred circle and to
> support one another in the process of letting go. As
> we let go of that which does not belong to us, or
> that which no longer serves us, we are lighter and
> liberated for the work of mapping the path
> forward. We honor the darkness, for it was surely
> illuminated by the light of love. We have lost a great
> light in our lives for whom we grieve. We

44

understand that while in the physical world, there was rarely enough time to deeply connect. Now, beyond the confines of the body, we are able to commune with her spirit without interruption. Lynn is no longer limited. Our beloved is not gone from us; she is right here in this sacred space and in our hearts. Her smile is brighter than this flame, and her laughter and her song are lifted upon smoke and breeze. The process of letting go allows us to pull her closer, as walls and barriers crumble and fall away.

As I led our circle through a guided visualization, we journeyed into an ancient passage tomb where we would become aware of all that we carried. Our goal now was to seek freedom and release. As we emerged into the light and back to our circle, we each took the time to write down every thought and realization discovered. We listed our regrets and our fears. We expressed our feelings of bitterness and sorrow, along with any words left unspoken. All to be carried to the expansive and ever present being of our dear one—no longer in human form. When every last word was written, they were carried to the flames and set alight with our heart's desire for transformation. Each page was burned into ash within a small stone basin, then carried to the water's edge. There, we symbolically cut cords attached to people who no longer would have ownership of our spiritual real estate. As we reached to the essence of water Herself—the Lady of the Lake—we asked for Her mercy and Her love to receive our words. All were cleansed and purified by fire, then blessed and consecrated by water—transformed and transmuted as dust became fluid.

We returned to the fire circle, shared stories, and sang songs—after all, this was one of Lynn's very favorite things—and then we concluded our work with these words:

With open hearts and untethered spirits, we cast our nets forth into the wisdom of all that is, anticipating the limitless abundance the Universe delivers with grace and ease, for which we are eternally grateful. And so, we are.

I know that our ceremony was blessed with great love and that the one that we can no longer see with our eyes remains ever present. She is in the garden with her love, she is at the fireside with dear friends, and she is sitting across from me as I write. Her laughter rises on billows of incense, and the flickering candle is the twinkle in her eye. It is not that we miss her any less than we did when the great void was opened that terrible day in Autumn, it is simply that we have chosen to carry her with us as we carry on. We were so blessed. We *are* so blessed!

The Once and Future Son – June 2018

At the end of 2015 my soul sister and childhood friend embarked on a healing journey. She is such a beacon of positivity and light that you would never know the darkness through which she has come. Her heart is so big and so open, you could not imagine that it had once been mishandled, manipulated, abandoned, and betrayed. Her generous heart just keeps shining, giving, expanding.

She is one of my great heroes and, without a doubt, a soul with whom I shall always resonate; together, we create a kind of harmony. She came into my life when we were ten years old and, though there have been separations of time and distance, when we come together, it feels as if no time has passed. Clearly, we are always together, hearts singing to one another over the miles.

Our favorite pastime is what we call "couch time." This is when and where we go deep. The season that her healing began brought us ample couch time, as she was staying with me while working on a project in town. She engaged the support of an intuitive life coach during this visit, and it was from her first session that our assignment was delivered.

I never wanted to have children of my own, though I've always been grateful for the faery goddess babies in my life. They are the sacred legacy of dearest friends who have nurtured my presence in the lives of their children. I've witnessed the joy, pride, and glory of motherhood through many of my girlfriends and I've witnessed the sorrow and heartbreak of some whose longing for such a blessing did not come to fruition. This is where our story begins.

Being separated by distance sometimes does not allow us to be witness to the suffering of loved ones. With 2,000 miles between us, I fear that, at the time, I was aware of my dear one's miscarriage but perhaps failed to be present with her loss and grief. I was grateful to have the opportunity to make up for my failure when she shared with me the task before her.

The very first mission of her healing journey was to make peace with the loss of her son. It was suggested that the work would be most powerful and effective at the Winter Solstice. It was early December and she was about to return home, but she asked me to help her with this endeavor and booked a flight to return for couch time later that month.

My own spiritual path of the last twenty-six years spirals around the Celtic wheel of the year. The significance of a ritual to greet her son on the day that the ancients celebrated the rebirth of the Sun felt like perfect timing. I set forth to create for her a sacred space in which to find celebration and closure.

The following meditation was inspired by my journey to Ireland in 2008. As I walked into the passage tomb known as *Newgrange* or *Brú na Bóinne*, it was clear to me that we were walking into the womb of Mother Earth. It can be seen from everywhere in the Boyne Valley, and this is where the people of this region would bring the cremated remains of their loved ones. There is a window box over the only doorway through which the rising sun enters only once a year—on the Winter Solstice.

It is my strong belief that they were longing for the return of their beloveds, along with the rebirth of the Sun. This is the time of year (in the Northern Hemisphere) we see the longest night, from which point the days begin to grow longer. This is the journey that my friend and I shared on the longest night of 2015.

The journey into darkness has been a long and difficult spiral inward. You have come to this place, upon a frosted, moonlit valley, to seek healing, comfort, and to lay down your burdens. In your mind's eye, you travel over the river . . . the surface alive with movement—spirals ascend as if to caress the face of the moon.

You journey upward, to that ancient place on the hill . . . the earthen mound that can be seen from anywhere in the valley . . . the womb of the Mother. As you approach, following the path that leads to the curb stone that marks the entrance, an Irish Hare pops up from the landscape, and dashes off, into the night. You arrive at the portal stone and run your fingers over the petroglyphs left upon the stone more than 5,000 years ago. These are clearly symbols of the river that brings bounty to this valley, and the cycle of life, death, and rebirth.

Now, you step forward and walk into the doorway. You are surrounded, as you move forward, by megalithic stones that form a passage of protective walls, and ceiling. It is dark here, and you step with intention, guided by the feel of the protective granite, but it is safe, and you can breathe with ease, knowing that you are held within the belly of the Mother. As the wall begins to curve, you know that you have reached the center . . . slightly up hill from the ground from which you entered. Here, you take a seat . . . and wait.

The Journey

On the longest night, you find peace in the darkness. You have come here to reconnect with the one you thought lost, the one who tried his best to come to fruition as the child of your womb... the son of your heart. It is here, in this ancient, sacred place . . . that you are finally able to give him a name. Here, before you, a shadowy image begins to emerge and take shape in the darkness. Outside, the very edge of the top of the sun is kissing the horizon, and a tiny ray of light has begun to journey toward you, across the cool stone floor. The pale light allows you to see that there is a large stone basin in the center of the chamber, and the small being that is emerging from the darkness is a young boy . . . who bears a striking resemblance to someone familiar.

As the light continues to gather in the chamber, you are able to see more clearly now. The boy before you holds out his hands, reaching for you. As you lean in . . . you feel the small, dry, warm palms upon each side of your face. As you look deeply into those eyes . . . your *eyes, gazing lovingly back at you . . . you are finally able to have that conversation that your soul has longed to share. Greet him by name . . . and take the time you need to speak with one another. Say the words that float from your heart to wrap him in mother's love . . . and wait to hear his reply. There is no need to rush, in this sacred place . . . you are both, for this moment . . . timeless.*

When words have been shared, tears have been shed, and laughter has tickled the tips of your toes . . . you look again, into those familiar, beautiful eyes that reflect all that is perfect in this world. You see the one who has never let you down. Recognizing yourself *as great warrior of your own story, you release the feeling of loss and sorrow, feeling in your heart, that it has been replaced by gratitude and joy.*

By now, the bottom of the sun has gently caressed the horizon, and its beams of pure, radiant, healing light are streaming through the window above the doorway to the passage. The altar stone, upon which your sacred child is seated, is enveloped with a golden light. As you gaze upon his beloved being, you gasp to realize that he *has become the light. Every inch of his body has begun to shimmer, like sparkling gold. He reaches for you again, and you take him into your arms for a final embrace.*

When you both have shared the comfort of touch, and are ready to say . . . farewell, for now . . . you loosen your grip, and his shimmering being pours through your body with a warming, glow of golden light. He has been released from this world, and his radiance leads you gently out of the ancient mound, and back into the full, warm light of the sun. It is a new day, and you feel refreshed and light. You are ready to emerge from the passage . . . and for the new opportunities that you shall bring to birth in the days and months ahead.

(I chanted a favorite piece by the Pagan group KIVA):

We are the earth.
We are the womb.
Come rising sun.
Lead us from the tomb.

Beautiful being . . .
Welcome to the light!

Through these words and upon this journey within, my friend found the closure she sought. She made peace with her sorrow and regret. She found a way to have a relationship with a soul that she cannot see but that surrounds her and moves her, despite the limitations of an earthly body. She asked me to share with my readers the message she received from her son, Izzy. As she looked down upon his face, he said to her, "Love yourself. Look at me, I look just like you. Love you as you would love me."

If you are aching for the loss of a loved one, whether or not you knew her or him in a form made manifest, know that my soul-sister and I are holding you close. We invite you to take this journey into yourself and there, we hope you may find comfort and deep peace. Love and brightest blessings shine brightly upon your sacred journey.

Mountain Music – July 2018

I am sitting on the porch of my friends' Tennessee home, and the breeze offers a slight chill as it plays with my hair while the lowering sun caresses my skin with warmth. A variety of birds are singing their evening songs, which speak of a beautiful day blessed by sunshine and the smell of sweet grass. Several are dancing around the nearby feeder, reminding me that the term "eats like a bird" doesn't mean what most people assume.

My friend lost his sweet mother last year, and this space that we are blessed to enjoy was lovingly referred to by that kind and generous woman as Mockingbird Cottage. Her gentle spirit still surrounds us in this heavenly place. I can sense that she is near, laughing at the hungry birds at play and recalling the way the wind once felt against her skin on a cool summer evening. She and I close our eyes and breathe deeply of this moment of shared peace and solitude. We anticipate the arrival of fireflies within the next hour.

I drove up on Friday, and the journey was pleasant. The companion I chose read to me his words of experience and wisdom with the voice of a philosopher. I downloaded required reading for my end-of-life doula coursework through Audible, and Stephen Jenkinson's voice fed my mind throughout my ten-hour journey. The book contained his thoughts on palliative care, called *Die Wise: A Manifesto for Sanity and Soul*. Eight hours of reading remains, and he has already given me so much to think about. He tells us about the way that death—though it is the one guarantee that comes with birth—is something that most people fear and run from. Many of his patients who chose palliative care, when a diagnosis became a prognosis, would later come to curse the effectiveness of their treatment. They discovered it was keeping them alive long past their wish to continue. In other words, it may have given them more time but it did not necessarily give them more "life;" just more suffering.

That kind of took my breath away. It made me think more clearly about the wording I would use in my advance directive, the official forms that will state my wishes for end-of-life care.

It also made me think about the act of dying and the choices one makes for how to spend their final days once a deadline has been given. And if one would choose to do things any differently, at that point (assuming the body was able), why we would wait until we've been given a deadline to start living in a way that would finally feed our soul. Should we not be spending all of our days that way? I mean, the day we are born, one thing that is certain is that we will also die. It seems to me that there is always a deadline, it's just that the expiration date is hidden beneath the fold of awareness.

I wonder what that might look like for me—a well-fed soul— and I believe that it looks something like sitting outside on a summer evening to hear the cacophony of birds chirping, cicadas humming, and distant dogs barking. It also looks like valuable time spent connecting with dear friends, and making new ones at a mountain art festival. It looks like smiling at the tiny green bug that just landed on the keyboard, finding rest until it is ready to take flight. It looks like taking the time to dive into a topic that once felt overwhelming and frightening, so that I may one day be of service in a way that transcends and ascends my former level and ability of caring. It looks like choosing to fill the rest of my days, be they long or few, with greater purpose and meaning.

Sitting here, in this sacred space outdoors, with the spirit of this sweet lady that I was blessed to know and shall always adore, I can list the messages that nature has delivered for my inability to hear her voice. The symbolism of the mockingbird is overcoming fear. The symbolism of the hummingbird, whose presence inspired the urge to write, is lightness of being and enjoyment of life as well as the reminder to be more present. The symbolism of the fireflies for whom we wait is self-illumination, guidance, and freedom.

As I glance over my shoulder to see if they have yet arrived, I see a cardinal at the feeder and smile to myself to realize that the symbolism of this particular bird is a reminder to realize the importance of your purpose in life . . . while for some, it informs them of the presence of a loved one lost. She knows I'm thinking of her and that I know she is here. That's affirmed by a glance before me to see that the cardinal has made his way across the darkening yard and stopped to look back at me from a moment's perch atop the umbrella nearby.

I am grateful for this time that I have given myself. I am able to explore the depths of my soul before stepping blindly into a new chapter that might be less than fulfilling (returning to a corporate role). I breathe deeply with gratitude for the beauty of nature, and for what we cannot see or hear without the courage to open our hearts. After all, love is not something visible; it can only be felt with the heart. So, I dare you, dear ones to close your eyes and open your hearts. There are messages flashing before you like the fireflies who have just arrived. I'd love for you to join me in this reverie of light and flight! Tell me . . . what do you see?

The Journey Inward – July 2018

Yesterday, I visited a nearby mountain park to get an added dose of nature before I head home at the end of the week. I hadn't really thought it out very well, because I stepped onto the Lakeside Trail in my traditional open-toe shoes instead of something more trail appropriate. I could have turned back early on, but the path kept calling me forward . . . and so forward I went. The "lake" was more of a reservoir and was not round like many lakes back home but more like a wide river with end caps. I started my journey, like most adventures in life, without expectation or awareness of what I might find or experience along the way. At the beginning of the trail, as I traveled counterclockwise on the map, I found a bench at water's edge, and so I sat for a moment to contemplate the beauty before me. The water was filled with all sorts of plant life, and there were trees that had fallen on the bank and into the lake that were left to become a part of the landscape, creating homes for the creatures that live there. As I sat there, I would occasionally hear a sound that informed me that something was moving in the water but each time I heard it, I would look and see nothing more than a slight ripple. It reminded me of how we often assume that a situation is how we perceive it based on what we can see on the surface, but how the reality is that there is often something of greater depth going on beneath it. I took a moment to honor all that was present that I could not see, and then I continued my walk.

Next, I came to a boardwalk structure that crossed the water and, before I was halfway across, I gasped to see a young deer with antlers grazing on plant life in shallow water. This is not something we get to see where I come from, and the sight took my breath away before it brought me to tears. A couple who was hiking in the opposite direction came upon us and respectfully stood quietly for a few minutes before gently passing by. I thought about how magick happens throughout our lives, if we are open to it, and how special it can be to have it all to ourselves at times, and also to be blessed to share it with others. I could have stayed all day simply to stand witness to such grace and beauty, but I decided to offer my gratitude for this moment, and asked to be *wowed* again somewhere along my journey. I was not disappointed.

As I moved forward on the path, with no idea where it would lead or if I would regret not turning back for better hiking gear, I couldn't help but think about my personal life experience with the Artemis archetype. After all, the stag is one of her most sacred symbols and the mountain forest is her realm. I might turn a curve along this winding path and see her in the distance drawing back her bow. I thought about how alone I felt on this path, as I could hear no human sound at this point. I realized that my footwear could betray me on a path filled with tree roots and loose stones, or how I might slip and fall somewhere on this journey and that no one would be around to see me, hear me, or come to my rescue.

It made me think about how unprepared I have been for the obstacles that would appear in my life, leaving me hurt or disappointed by the actions of others. But then, I realized that my travels with Artemis have always been that way. I may have had the support of my band of nymphs that I call my tribe, but the work that I did to move through self-loathing to find my true self-worth and value was always a solitary journey. It never mattered how emphatically others would assure me of how worthy they found me; I could never find it to be true until I felt it for myself. And every betrayal and wound I've received has always led to learning and the positive evolution of my soul. And so . . . I chose to continue, believing that I was well protected and that I would find more moments of magick if I simply refused to give up on myself.

As I moved further into the forest, and away from view of the lake, the feeling of solitude grew more profound. I realized how similar this world that belongs to Artemis resembles the world that belongs to Persephone. In the non-patriarchal version of her tale, she has chosen to go into the underworld to welcome the souls who have transitioned from the world of the living and are now seeking passage through the veil. On this lonely mountain path, I could feel the isolation of one's journey from human form into the mystery of what comes next. There might be loved ones present to hold your hand for a while, but at some point . . . you must move forward on your own. I realized, through much of my hike that I heard a recurring sound that lacked form. I imagined that it might be the sound of hooves on forest floor, an unseen squirrel or chipmunk, or a bird taking flight in the canopy above.

The message that I received from this awareness was that our perception of aloneness throughout our sacred journey is an illusion. Even when we cannot see others around us, the truth is that we are never alone. When strength rises within us, we are filled with the unseen force of the warrior archetype. When peace settles within us, it is the mother archetype that arrives to deliver comfort. And perhaps on the days when we are feeling abandoned, we may feel the presence of our lost loves walking beside us. These energies are at once surrounding us and moving through us. We are all one.

As I walked the Lakeside Trail, wondering if it would ever come to an end, I walked through fear and kept going. I walked through solitude and realized I wasn't alone. I walked through self-doubt and negative self-talk about the foolishness of being ill-prepared, and I kept moving forward. I walked for three hours straight, and never grew weary. I acknowledged that my twice-weekly time in the gym had been time well spent, as my legs were strong enough to carry me up hill and down again without complaint. I passed an occasional human and while I was glad to see them and smiled as they passed, I was also grateful to continue on my own.

I realized that walking with Artemis brought me to this place where being alone with myself is a wonderful place to be. Once filled with self-loathing, I now feel that I make for great company and I was so happy to be walking with my own best friend . . . *me*.

As I began to hear traffic on the mountain road where I entered the park, I was pleased to come full circle. I had hoped to be shown the blessings of nature and I was rewarded with three different deer sightings, each bringing me to tears. For three hours, I was honored to walk beside two Goddesses who are ever-present in my life. I bowed my head to Persephone in reverence for the guidance and comfort she provides as I explore the path to the underworld. I hope to be one of her torchbearers in the future, holding the hands of those transitioning from human form until they are finally able to see those who shall greet them on the other side.

The Enlightened Heart – August 2018

One thing has been a delightful surprise and an enormous blessing about this journey of discovery through end-of-life studies. I am grateful for the willingness and courage displayed by others who have been moved to share their own stories of loss.

The required reading provides stories from the perspective of hospice doctors, nurses, and palliative care providers. But the truth shared by a friend of their own experience as a witness to a loved one's departure is far more meaningful to me. These sacred moments of vulnerability and raw emotion are so deeply personal. I consider it a great honor and privilege to be given the opportunity to hold space and bear witness, not to the dying in these cases, but to those who remain. I feel as if I have been offered a gift from a friend who shares their experience. It is a reflection of grace that might just be a guide for me when my darkness comes.

At the end of our days upon the earth, the path onward splits as the survivor has no choice but to step forward in a new direction while they create their new normal. What a privilege to see how sorrow leads to strength, and strength leads to becoming in the heart of a friend surviving the loss of a love.

The one who has died has given up their earthly belongings, and those who love them have lost the physical presence of someone dear. These moments are woven into the tapestry of our individual mythology and they are important tales of our own evolution. I am honored to hold these sacred moments in the light of truth and with the warmth of love.

I just finished reading the fourth and final book of required reading for this course, *The Tibetan Book of Living and Dying* by Sogyal Rinpoche. If you are interested in reading it and enjoy audiobooks, I found it on YouTube. I find that spoken words allow pieces that feel important to me to rise and then I can find them in the book and deepen my focus where I have been drawn.

Within the six and a half hours of listening, I found my draw at the halfway point . . . just over three hours in. Interestingly, the first three hours were on the topic of living, while the last three hours were on dying, death, and rebirth. These pages are filled with pathways to compassion. They offer instruction through meditation—which kind of speaks my language.

A side note and extended interlude on my own journey with meditation and practice:

> *I remember the first time I tried to meditate. It was 1992, and I was taking a class on Wicca. Ken Windwalker had a passion for meditation and offered a Saturday morning practice. I remember sitting on the floor of a darkened room, receiving soothing guidance with eyes closed. When we were instructed to open our eyes at the end, I was simply frustrated. We were going around the room, each person sharing what they had visualized on their journey within . . . and let me tell you these visions were magickal. As for myself, however, I felt that I had failed to go anywhere and simply could not push the mundane out of my mind.*
>
> *Windwalker asked me what I had seen, and the truth was that I was balancing my checkbook in my mind. Ugh . . . nothing spiritual about that. He asked me to close my eyes and prompted me to say aloud what I could see. I can't remember the results of that exercise, but I could see*

that there was potential if I could just get out of my own way.

It was after Ken died that my tribe dedicated a year to meditation. Each week, we gathered and rotated responsibility for sharing a meditation with the group. At this point in time, our lack of experience led us to share meditations written by others. It was a year well-spent, because at some point I did finally get out of my way and learned to travel. I offer gratitude for this accomplishment to my friend and teacher, who surely helped guide me there, remaining an unseen force in my life years after his passing.

The art of compassion and how to serve is the foundation of the Buddhist structure shared within the pages of this book; a temple of healing with the power of the mind. We are reminded to touch the suffering of another with love rather than fear. Fear leads to pity, while love leads to compassion. To activate and mentally direct this compassion, we may consider the following:

Close your eyes and take a deep cleansing breath. Visualize a green light coming through your breath and into your heart, where it brightens and expands with each rise and fall of your chest. As this light shines more brightly, it illuminates the wise ones who surround you. You may see them and name them as your own spiritual path allows, be they ascended masters, angels, guides, God, Universal Energy, Spirit, ancestors, etc. Ask for their guidance to allow your words, thoughts, and actions only to benefit and bring happiness to others—to support their transformation from suffering to peace. Direct the compassion you possess, by positive action and spiritual practice, to the dedication of the welfare and enlightenment of all beings. Know that your own attainment of these goals will be for the benefit of all. And with this breath of compassion and enlightenment—we breathe in the sorrow and suffering of others, and we breathe out kindness. We breathe in the panic and fear that surrounds us, and we breathe out happiness.

The black smoke of suffering is replaced with the green light of the enlightened heart. The art of *Tonglen* is to transmute pain and suffering by giving and receiving. I receive your suffering and give you my happiness. I receive your grief and I give you my peace of mind. All of this occurs through the breath. This is a simplified explanation of the practice that is detailed in *The Tibetan Book of Living and Dying*. I feel that a daily practice will be developed from these pages and I hope that my heart light may be a comfort to you when you are in need.

Like my teacher before me, I have gone on too long. Know that you are loved, and that I am grateful to have you walking beside me.

Your Light Required – September 2018

On a normal day devoted to writing, I typically sit down at the keyboard, empty my mind, and ask for inspiration to come. Words flow from my fingertips without a conscious direction. My writing is a mystery that is revealed to me as it comes. It reminds me of the metaphor my soul-daughter has used for my current path; she says that I am on a long, dark highway and I can only see what is illuminated by my headlights. The road is safe, my GPS is leading me to where I need to be, and my car is safe with a full tank of gas. All that is required is to keep driving forward, pay attention to what is being revealed as I go, and know that I will be informed when it is time to stop driving.

On these days that I am focused on writing, I am often reaching into my past for a story to tell, through which some level of insight or self-healing may be revealed. Today is different. Today, I am writing about something from my future, and I'd like to engage your support. I promise that it will not cost you more than a moment of thought, and what I know for sure is that the light produced by your mindful awareness will add to the light of mine, and together we may just permeate the darkness descending upon a sacred soul. Now, the soul of whom I write is specific, but together—our reach may be broader. Each of us may be just a drop of quenching rain, but together we can be a monsoon of healing light, a tsunami of love.

The holy one who I write about is the beloved sister of a dear friend. In this year of transformation, she has selflessly offered her gifts to me, as she does to anyone in need, asking for nothing more than the pleasure of my company in return. She, herself, is a warrior of overcoming—and she has reached to me with a request to grab my bow and lead this tribe of loved ones through a circle of healing. The invading predator is fierce; ALS invades the body and robs it of its strength to move, and eventually . . . to breathe.

You see, this is why I need you today and your stunning, radiant inner light. My love is great and enveloping, but *our* love? It is all consuming, a cloak of comfort on a cold dark night. Please take my hand and share your light. I can see it growing brighter as you approach, and it is sweetness to behold; love made manifest. Further, I hope you would not consider it greedy to ask that you share this post with others. Imagine the power of our light when it is passed from one sacred soul to another! We are each torchbearers, passing our light from one to another until the whole world is aglow with a radiance more powerful than the sun.

For the purposes of our focused connection, I am going to refer to our sacred vessel as Juno. For clarity, if you are reading this after the date of this gathering to which you are contributing, know that time is not linear and your light will still make a difference. Also, understand that if you are in need of healing light, you may pull it from this cosmic gathering, and when you offer your own healing energy you are never depleted, for this is a divine force that moves through you; you cannot help but receive through the giving.

Great Spirit, Mother/Father God, Universal Force of Creation, Powers that Be, Elements that surround us and flow through us, All That Is; allow this sacred circle of beautiful beings to become a combined vessel of your love, filling up and spilling forth with an abundance of healing light energy. Allow the light of love to flow freely, without obstacle, and let it drip down the healer's hands, washing away our sorrows, our fears, our hunger, and thirst, our aches and pains, self-doubt, and false limitations. As we are made of celestial matter, we contain the healing power of a thousand suns, and the distant light of a billion stars is ever present in the combustive force that warms us from within.

Let this divine energy rise up through Earth's core and crust, through saline ocean, and forest floor, through the soles of our feet, rising up through the roots that are our legs, lighting up our energetic being as it is filled—(red) root, (orange) sacral, (yellow) solar, and into our (green) hearts contained by strong and resilient trunks, and let this molten, healing light flow through arms to hands that are our branches, through (blue) throat, (purple) mind's eye that sees what is not visible, and (white) crown—through that, which we connect easily with all that is . . . rising up and out to deliver exactly what is required, be it for the good of all. Amen, So Be It, Blessed Be.

If it is difficult to connect with the soul of someone you do not yet know, think of someone you do know who has made you feel completely loved. Hold that beloved being in your heart and radiate and reflect that love back to her or him. As you feel that radiance shared between the two of you, allow that light to expand to encapsulate others in your circle—family and friends for who you feel a sense of affection. Now, expand that light even further, beyond those you know well and out to acquaintances, and then to people you don't know in your community, in your city, in your state. Let your light of loving compassion grow and spread beyond the boundaries of country, continent, planet. Let your love reach and grow into the darkness of space, surrounding the galaxy, and then every galaxy—known and unknown. Know that your light is expansive and boundless. You are one with the Universe and all that is.

Now, bring your focus back into your center. Visualize this place that is in a realm not limited by what we know in this world. In this place, there is plenty of room for all of us to gather. We are each standing in our own strength, prepared to share it freely with one another. If you once felt alone in this space, feel the arrival of other light beings, as the palms of your hands are filled with the palms of two others.

As each of us arrive in this sacred circle, a pale blue light radiates from each being and as hands are linked, the light begins to pulsate and grow stronger as it flows gently in a clockwise motion from heart to heart and hand to hand. As the circle is made complete, you look before you and see Juno seated at the center, enveloped in the pale blue light of your loving presence. Let Juno be represented by that being who has made you feel most loved and cherished and let that love be reflected back to her.

She is surrounded by Universal light delivered through sacred souls from all over the planet. You may be holding hands with someone from America, from Canada or Ireland, from India or from Africa; your light is mingling with the light of people from countries whose names have never crossed your lips. We are all one, and there are no barriers here. We are all here for one purpose; to bring divine healing light to the soul of another, in whatever form is needed. When we offer our healing energy—Reiki, Theta, our thoughts and prayers—it must be unattached to outcome, for we cannot know the destined journey of one's soul. We can only trust that exactly what is needed to bring healing to that sacred soul, in any form, will be delivered by our care.

As the light surrounding Juno grows and pulsates, it is like a magnet pulling from her body; any residue of past harm, be it betrayal, fear-based thought, denial of success or personal worthiness, food-born or environmental distress or illness. As all remnants of negativity and disease (mentioned and unnamed) are removed from her body, her energetic being, her DNA, and her beautiful soul—all areas of exit are filled and sealed with golden light.

The pale blue light, which has grown in strength as each new soul enters the circle, becomes a beautiful emerald green. As Juno has been emptied of what no longer serves her, she has become an open vessel to receive the light that we offer as well as the sparkly white light of creation that flows from above. We are a grateful witness to the arrival of this light and are awed by the beauty that illuminates Juno's own beauty. She is filled with this light that is like the golden light from a holiday sparkler, or a downpour of luminous glitter. This light fills every cell of her body with divine healing energy as it delivers strength and fortitude for the road ahead. Juno receives through her open heart the wisdom of the Universe, the strength of earthly ancient mountains, the air to fill her lungs and speak her truth, the fire to move her muscles and accomplish every task she seeks to fulfill, the water to wash her spirit clean of fear, anger, bitterness, and regret.

Juno is filled with divine light and soothed by the love that surrounds her. Whatever is required for her peace, comfort, and transformation in the form that her soul has chosen will be provided with grace and ease. She is one with all of us and we are all one with the Universe. Together, we transcend the limitations beholden to the confines of the human body through the power of the mind, which is greater than our understanding. Once again, we place our trust within this truth that assistance is given to those who reach. Together, we reach beyond what we can see, feel, understand, and know that this mystery is received and freely given through the love that resides within each of us.

Finally, in this sacred place where we have gathered, we raise our hands toward Juno and send golden light energy from heart to palm and into her being. She will carry the love of this circle within her through all of her days upon the earth and into the mystery of what comes next.

And when you feel that you have given what she needs, place your hands upon your own heart and receive that same energy that flows through you and each sacred being within this circle. Allow your own body and energetic being to be filled with this Universal Light Energy. Feel the light and love of this vast community surround you and enter your heart. Know that you carry this love within you, and that it seeps through every pore with a radiant light that brings healing to old wounds and attracts an abundance of goodness to your life.

When you are ready to return to the place where you are sitting, reading these words that have somehow come through my fingertips and onto this page, I hope that you hold onto my gratitude and my love for the light that you have offered and for the healing it has provided. You are loved and valued beyond your previous imagining. Hold onto that and let it grow in your awareness. Your light will illuminate your path, and beauty surrounds you, every step of the way.

Thank you! I love you! It is done!

PS: Should you, or someone you love, ever be in a place where our light may be required, please place that sacred being where Juno now sits, and know that this sacred ceremony was written for this very moment. You can help. We can help. Somehow, in a place beyond our understanding, we shall rise—warriors, all!

More than Grateful – September 2018

Last night, I had dinner with one of my soulmates. You've met him already—my friend Brian.

Over our shared meal, Brian told me that the oncologist had given him until summer to live. So we clinked our toast to one another just days before the autumn equinox, conscious of this great blessing.

Brian shared with me that he is working twelve-hour days. It is thankless work that brings him no joy, save for our dinners when he comes to town. I argue that a corporation that would require an employee who is immunocompromised to get on a plane once a month would be complicit in his future decline. Still, I am grateful for each time that he lands in my city.

My darling friend longs for laughter, which once was a daily ritual—and I feel he should have it! Having recently learned from my financial advisor that I can collect a monthly income from my IRA without penalty until I turn fifty-nine, I asked my friend his age. He declared that he had never shared his true age with anyone, but then confessed that he is already at an age where he can collect those funds, as well as social security. Further, he noted that his mortgage is paid in full.

In other words, the only reason for him to sacrifice his valuable time to a corporation is for the fear of requiring health care. One of the important notes within my end-of-life doula studies is about the blessing of hospice care. I'm pretty sure that this is the one good thing to come from my friend's prognosis; when one is given six months to live, they automatically qualify for hospice care. I think people fear engaging such care because it might feel like a statement to the Universe that they are giving up on life. I wholly disagree. Consider that one might engage hospice for the care that is their right to receive while living in one of the wealthiest countries on the planet. Then one might set out to defy the prognosis of one's disease. Hospice will see you reach the six-month mark, and adjust their sails to get you all the way home when the time is right.

So, I have challenged my soulmate to go home and do his research, and then to make himself his own priority. His husband is already doing so.

I told him that when he retires, he won't be coming to my city for work anymore . . . so I would simply have to come to him. He has important work ahead of him, but not for the benefit of a corporation. His number one care holder, deserves every ounce of his energy, every moment of his valuable time, and every rise of his laughter. He will relish the blessing of being of service to the one person he holds most dear. May there be an abundance of days left to share.

My soulmate tells me that each time he sees me, he is filled with renewal and hope as I provide sustenance to ponder. The funny thing is, were it not for his presence in my life, none of this wisdom would have been available to me. Had my empathic heart not been introduced to his courageous soul, the past year of my life might not have been spent in deep contemplation of my own joy and happiness. Though I still am unsure of where this path will lead, I know for certain that learning more about death has taught me way more about life. It is meant to be filled with love, light, laughter, and joy and when there is suffering, it is meant to be honored, comforted, held in reverence, and soothed by love. The blessing of Brian's extended stay in my life leaves me feeling more than grateful.

Make a Wish – September 2018

Hello, dear friend. Tonight, there will be a celebration in your honor. It's your birthday, and not one among us would miss the opportunity to give thanks for your birth. Your beloved has been working hard on the setting and it shall be a glorious sight. Last night, we put finishing touches on the Harry Potter corner; a tip of the Sorting Hat to your love of those powerful stories of friendship, steadfastness, and the ultimate message of love overcoming fear—always. Tibetan prayer flags have been hung to allow the wind to carry our prayers to you. Before they are lifted to the heavens, the prayer-filled breeze will surely dance with the lush plants and flowers of your memorial garden.

We cannot believe that ten months have passed since your body left us. It's a funny thing for those of us who didn't get to see you often to contemplate this reality, especially when we feel even closer to you than when you were here. I believe you have been walking with me, in your own mystical way, since that perfectly wonderful eleven-and-a-half-hour day we shared in the hospital last October. Do you remember? It carries such a crisp beauty in my mind's eye; your radiant smile brightened not just the room, but the whole hospital and, surely, the whole world.

What a delight it was for me to have you *all* to myself.

Our future journey together didn't exactly turn out as we had planned, did it? But you know . . . I think it is turning out okay, after all. I didn't get to help you make your dreams come true, but I get to be witness to your beloved doing so. She is following your lead, and I know that you are enormously proud of her. You taught me about healing through grace and she is teaching me about healing through gratitude.

Like many other things that have occurred this year, I am certain you have played a role in the deepening of our friendship. We are both on this journey of leaving behind a path that shifted beneath our feet, leaving us breathless, and then enlightened. We have finally figured out that time is precious and it need not be neglected. It is up to us to give it our love, attention, and devotion. The time that we have upon the earth is sacred and we have work to do. But not the kind of work that is thankless and unkind. The work before us is all about filling the time we have with more joy, more light, more love, more togetherness, more laughter, more remembrance.

So, here we are—gathered together—not in sorrow, but in joy. Our souls dance to the music that you planted within our hearts. Without you here, we may not remember the words but we can hum along. Our eyes are closed, our chins lifted, with our ears cupped for the hopeful capture of your crisp, beautiful voice upon evening breeze. Tonight, we, this gathering of intentional family bound by love, will light the candles of your birthday *pie*. Though you will not have the breath to blow them out, we know that your wish has already come true. Beloved Lynn, we love you most!

Into the Fire – September 2018

Wow! What a wonderful whirlwind weekend. It was filled with festivity and fire—oh—and retirement. It's not exactly what you think. At forty-nine, I'm a long way from actual retirement in the traditional sense. When I reached out to the financial planner that is enabling my friend's retirement at age fifty-nine-and-a-half, I certainly had no idea that he could do anything for me in the immediate future. But when I expressed to him that I had exited the corporate world last year and how I felt that I could never return, he offered a suggestion.

He said that my hard-earned savings could start working for me now. There is apparently a provision provided by the IRS called 72T. It was utilized a great deal when the market crashed and jobs became scarce. It enabled those who had to take lower paying jobs to access their retirement savings, without penalty, to receive a monthly income from their IRA until they reached retirement age. It only allows a small percentage, but could provide the opportunity for someone who lives rather simply to focus on, oh, say . . . becoming a writer, without having to sell her soul back to the corporate world.

Once that exciting new beginning was set in motion, it was time to focus on the important stuff; the celebration of our beloved Lynn. It was time to celebrate what would have been her sixty-eighth birthday. So, her wife and I went shopping to create the festive atmosphere that would express the spirit of our bountiful harvest of gratitude. We don't really experience the beauty of autumn here in Florida the way that states north of us do. In fact, our fall won't come until February when the oak trees drop their dark green leaves and replace them with fresh canopy of light green. So, we decorate on the inside while the outside insists that we remain in the season of summer.

Lynn would have loved her birthday celebration on Saturday. The atmosphere, the intention, the music, and most importantly, the people. It was a small gathering of thirteen, a tiny fraction of those who loved our girl. We gathered, we shared a meal, we each wrote love notes to Lynn on strips of paper that were rolled up and dropped into a bottle of orange glass. She loved the color orange, and we loved getting to tell her what we loved about her and how she made us feel. Through this ritual we sent her our communal "message in a bottle" as another form of prayer and gratitude. We each spoke of our memories of one of our favorite healers, about how we fell in love with her upon meeting, how she sang to us around the campfire, how she taught us to be better people, how she listened with rapt attention and made us feel completely heard, and better—understood.

We sat in awe of how she expressed to us that her weeks in the hospital, as friends came from all over just to sit with her, were the happiest weeks of her life. And we cried. Some tears were certainly from the sorrow of our great loss, and for her physical absence. But—to be clear—most of our tears were joyful, for the glory of having been blessed to have Lynn in our lives and to still feel her presence, to this day. When stories were shared, we blessed them with song. Two guitars, two dulcimers, one ukulele, one tuba, and one rain stick, along with thirteen voices made up our chorus for the angel who used to lead our choir.

None of us could do what she could do to lead a campfire circle of song, but we tried . . . and we could feel her smiling upon us as we read lyrics from cell phones. She was the keeper of words and without her, we simply have to make do. We had pie, and her grandsons blew out her birthday candles, knowing that her wish had come true in our togetherness. We finished the evening with creativity . . . manifesting our love and light through acrylic pour. She would have loved the way that you simply allow the color to flow onto the canvas and become what it becomes—without judgment or doubt, just appreciation. After all, that's how she felt about each of us.

On Sunday, I returned to help with clean up and relaxation. The autumn equinox is a time of balance, when day and night are equal, and it is also a time for harvest. When I consider my personal harvest this year, I find it filled with more bounty than I could have imagined. I think I'll save that declaration for another post, but I will tell you that the deepening of this friendship and being blessed to witness the grief, wisdom, and joy of my friend as she journeys forward from the loss of her beloved is at the top of my list.

Together, we discussed the beauty of Saturday's gathering and how we could feel Lynn's presence. We cried as friends and loved ones sent messages acknowledging the important date, and how she was remembered far and wide. Together, we shared leftovers with gratitude for the sustenance the Earth provides. And by the time we were either ready to head our separate ways for a nap or go deep into healing, we chose healing.

I spoke of nightmares and thoughts of past betrayals (personal and work-related) that had recently been plaguing my heart and mind. I wondered why they were emerging at this moment, when I felt I was ready to move forward. My friend had her own sense of obstacles that were ready for removal, and she had discovered a useful tool through a meditation app we use called Insight Timer.

The meditation was a shamanic journey called Rise of the Phoenix by Dakota Earth Cloud, and it was possibly the most powerful meditation/ritual I've experienced. It was more than a meditation because my friend built a fire and we called in the elements and Great Spirit from Native American tradition. We called in our guides, our ancestors, and our late loved ones. I could see the determined and supportive faces of my grandparents, my Aunt Beth, Windwalker, and—of course—our Lynn. When the fire was blazing and we were about to begin, I fed the names of my offenders to the flames. Not in a way that would be harmful or destructive to any of them, four women and four men, but in a way that would be transformative and healing. "Thank you for teaching me, I release these lessons and any need for more through the experience of betrayal—I trust myself now. Go in peace." By Dakota's lead, this is what I saw in that dimension where the mind takes you when you step away from the mundane and into the mystery.

I entered the portal to this dimension through one of my favorite entryways, a cave. When I go there, I start at the edge of a clear water lake atop a mountain where I swim through the reflection of the stars above, downward into the mouth of an underwater crystal cave. I made my way through safe passage by torchlight and when the path split, I went left (as I often do). I was met by my guides whom I call the Sacred Fourteen, and they surrounded me as I stepped into the fire that was burning in the center of the space. From there, I called out the names of those who had let me down. There were three bosses and one female friend, three lovers and one male friend, and as I finally expressed how I had been wounded—I yelled in spirit for how angry I was that they would put me in a situation where I would feel badly about myself, opening a wound where self-loathing and doubt would take root.

The breath of fire and a shamanic drumbeat raised the energy for transformation and as I yelled on the inside, I sobbed on the outside. I turned my head to the left to inhale through my nose, tapped my left foot, grabbed with my left hand (the side of the body that represents the past) and then turned my head to the right to exhale through my mouth, tapped my right foot, released with my right hand (the side of the body that represents the future), and I pulled up and spit out nearly forty years of contained anguish.

At this point, Dakota instructed us to ask our guides for help with this healing fire, and the Sacred Fourteen stepped in closer, and raised their arms to strengthen the impassioned flame to completely consume me. And as the roots of destruction were pulled from my being and burned away by these flames, I noticed that others had stepped in. To take the place of three bosses who betrayed me came three bosses who loved me through it all (and still do). To take the place of friends who left through shame, mutual hurt, and confusion came friends who stayed and stepped up to help me heal. To take the place of men who had cheated, abandoned, stolen, and lied came men who had proven to me with action and presence that it is not *all* men who cannot be trusted.

As I cried tears of sorrow, my friend's dog, Maggie, leapt into my lap, licked my tears, and settled into my embrace. She stayed until my tears turned to those of joy. Surrounded by so much loving support, including that of my friend—standing within her own fire—adding to my healing flame with her intention, I felt the flames burn clean. There was no more debris to be cleared; all that remained was the light of my blue-white wings as I rose like the phoenix. As I looked down upon the circle of my healing, I recognized the faces of my love with gratitude.

As if she knew exactly when the magick would be complete, Dakota invited us to leave this sanctuary the way we came in . . . and so I did. Only this time, I was carried out in triumph by the Sacred Fourteen. They joyfully delivered me through corridor, now lit by my flaming wings, and to the edge of the cavern. I thanked them and turned to swim upward through clear mountain lake, and rose above the water and into the stunning night sky. When we found ourselves back in our chairs by the fire's edge with our feet in the grass, my friend and I clasped hands and thanked each other. We were both aware of the work that we had done for each other, but more importantly, for ourselves.

Great Spirit, thank you. It is done. Blessed be. Aho!

Careholder – October 2018

I remember in my past life—the one that revolved around a stressful role in a corporate office—that each time I took an overdue vacation, it would take me a few days to finally feel disconnected from the intensity and worry of what was happening in the workplace. Especially in those last few years that were tainted by layoffs and the hostile takeover of the board of directors, which were sources of extreme pressure for those I served. Gratefully, I ventured forth from my new normal and into a vacation with friends last week, free from that kind of stress . . . but I must confess that it has taken me a few days to shake free from worry.

My new worry lies with care and concern for my aging parents. It is difficult to disconnect from this particular source of anxiety, for it is far more important than any corporate or executive angst. I don't think I'm alone in my lack of complete presence this week, for I know that each of us on this journey carries a similar weight. One of my friends may be speaking, and I am running a movie of whether my father is comfortable or my mother has received the care she needed for her aching knee. I can personally recall the way that my parents jumped to action when I was sick or hurting and now it is my father who is hurting. At eighty-one, a blister on the foot from lack of socks with shoes can become a dangerous wound requiring antibiotics and daily treatment . . . and a bedsore? Ugh!

One of my life lessons has been the overcoming of fear-based thought. I have been fearful of never being loved enough. I have feared losing the job that provided security. I have feared the suffering of beloved pets, and if I prolonged their suffering selfishly. I have feared gaining back weight that was so very difficult to lose. I have feared injury that I might not recover from.

All of these things were major challenges to conquer in the field of thought, especially since we tend to manifest what we think about. The comfort and safety of my parents exceeds all these concerns. It is heartbreaking to know that these people who have been powerful providers of love and support are facing the betrayal of their bodies and that there is little I can do to make it better. After all, this is life.

I would give anything to be able to wave my magic wand and erase memory loss or the sense of panic that comes when landmarks are not as remembered, and one feels lost. I would trade the contents of my 401K to ease your suffering and make your body strong again. I would wrap you in a cloak of comfort until you felt safe and knew that you would never fall down again.

If I could, I would hold you in my arms and rock you to sleep each night to help you feel whole and loved unconditionally. I know that I cannot make everything right again, for this is the path we must each travel. The body is not meant to go on forever, that is the task of the eternal soul; alas flesh is temporary. But love . . . love *is* forever. I will love you through every challenge you face. I will love your memory, even when it only recalls the disappointment and rarely the beauty. I will love your heart that has loved me for all of my days upon the earth, and the days before my feet ever touched the ground.

All of that corporate chaos from my personal history book is rendered obsolete in every future chapter. The time has come to nurture my most important shareholders. I hope not to let them down. But first, just a few more days of vacation. I love you most!

Acorn Becomes the Oak – October 2018

I have found myself in such an interesting place in recent months. I had heard the term before from friends whose parents were aging and required a bit more attention and care. While I don't want to say that I am becoming the parent to my parent—I have to admit, it feels like we are moving into a sort of role reversal.

My sweet Pop has lived eighty of his eighty-one years with epilepsy, and in the last ten years it has really taken a toll on his body. I call it body betrayal, the way that simple commands the body once executed with barely a thought, suddenly (or gradually) become tasks that require serious concentration and a concerted physical effort to perform. In 2008, Pop spent a good part of the year traveling to and from Mayo Clinic in Jacksonville. Test after test failed to reveal what was causing symptoms, which impaired his ability to walk, to feel his feet and fingertips, and eventually his ability to find words while speaking. I will never forget the day he told me that he was deeply depressed and that he didn't think he would live out the year. I was heartbroken, but I was also still working in a high-demand, stressful job in the corporate world, which didn't leave me with much time or energy to be of service.

Finally, he saw a local neurologist who reviewed the same lab results that Mayo Clinic ordered and reviewed, and my beloved father was diagnosed with a serious B-12 deficiency. Apparently, his epilepsy medication, his age, and the fact he was living with a vegetarian had left him seriously depleted. I later learned from a friend whose pediatrician had the same diagnosis, that if it had not been discovered he would have ended up in a coma. The end result of this oversight for such a length of time was permanent nerve damage and neuropathy in his feet, and from a lifetime of small seizures down his left side.

So, Poppy has been using a walker to get around for the last ten years, and he and Mom moved closer to me a few years ago. I'd never really imagined living seven houses away from my parents, but I have to tell you that I am really glad to have them nearby. I worry less than when they were forty-five minutes away with no neighbors around to check on them. I don't necessarily stop in every day, but I can glance over on the way to my house to be sure all appears well and can be there in two minutes if they call for assistance.

Yesterday, he finally followed instructions and remembered to call me when he got out of the walk-in tub. I can't say we loved the installation process, but we love that Dad can get in and out of a hot soak relatively well now. He said, "I'm out of the tub. You'd better hurry over before my toenails turn back to steel!" And within two minutes, I was serving at the feet of one of my heroes in his pajama bottoms, with my reading glasses (for protection as much as for magnification) and a pair of industrial strength clippers. I made sure the talons were shortened enough, then applied lotion before putting on his socks.

Next, I helped him put his shirt on and giggled as I exclaimed, "There he is!" as his head popped through the neck hole. (He's a pretty good sport about it all.) I finished up my service by brushing his hair, and made him a bagel with cream cheese.

I am not sure what I thought this time in our lives would have entailed, but I'm sure I might have imagined it to be sad or tedious, but so far it is not. For me, right now . . . it is joyful. I am one of the lucky ones, to have a father who is warm, kind, and generous to all who are blessed to know him. He was a social worker who served the physically handicapped for over thirty years, after all. I don't know if he imagined that some of the tools that he made available to his clients all those years ago, would be something my mom and I would be seeking for his comfort decades later.

Beyond any luxury that this year of freedom from the corporate world has given me, the freedom to care for my father and be present for my parents is my favorite most sacred thing. I'm so grateful to have them in my life, to have them nearby, and to have this time to show them my love, my affection, and to be of service when the future feels shorter and less certain than they've previously known. I hope they know that every single day they are loved.

Walking the Labyrinth – A Path to Healing, A Metaphor for Life – October 2018

My parents and I walked through Chartres Cathedral during a tour of the French countryside in the summer of my sixteenth year. It was a part of a month-long vacation that would take us through England and Scotland, as well. I was terribly homesick at times, but certain that I would later appreciate this opportunity I'd been given.

Indeed, that first introduction to the world of my ancestors left an indelible mark, and it would be revealed to me again and again, over the following decades. At the unfolding of my spiritual journey, it would rise to the surface like blue woad on the skin of ancient warriors.

A labyrinth is sometimes imagined to be a scary place, like the final challenge in Harry Potter's *Goblet of Fire* tournament, but in truth it can be a tool to assist you on a mindful journey within. These challenging mazes of film, like the scary winter scene in Steven King's *The Shining* are encapsulated by high walls that create a sense of isolation and sometimes panic as you become the player on a board game, taking each turn in hope to find freedom. The version that I refer to is a labyrinth that is simply marked upon the ground; a diagram that your feet will carry you through.

If we were witness to the labyrinth in Chartres Cathedral all those years ago, I have no memory of it. My first introduction to the concept was when a replica was painted on canvas and rolled out in an open space at my local Unitarian Church.

As I stood barefoot at the edge of this sacred cloth, I was informed that this was a tool for healing. Into the path we could carry our woes, and out of it we could carry a sense of hope. There is a single entrance and the path before us is wide enough to safely hold our footfalls, but there are many curves and turns that require our focus and attention. For this reason, when we carry an intention onto the path, we enter into a walking meditation.

It was the early 90s, and I had only recently been introduced to the art of meditation, so quieting my mind and finding clarity or focus was not yet one of my strengths. Walking the labyrinth at that time was an experience that I enjoyed and longed to do again, though its magick would grow stronger with time as the metaphor of the journey took shape in my life.

The next labyrinth I found was marked in stone in the yard of a retreat center in Asheville, North Carolina. Members of my tribe and I stepped onto the path, one by one, and moved forward and back, round and round. We were focused on the path for fear of tripping over the rocks of containment, and it felt as if we were walking alone. But as we moved in circles, our paths would sometimes meet and we would walk side by side, sharing the journey.

This is how our lives have been. At times, we feel alone with our personal struggles or daily dramas and then we are delighted to look up and realize that we were never alone at all. Members of our tribe may be at different edges of this winding road, but when we need them, or they need us, we need only stop for a moment to look up from the obstacles that threaten our stability and find their reassuring smiles surrounding us. From here, we know that we can keep moving forward.

For a long time, the art of the labyrinth was elusive. It was something found on travel, or special occasion. But today, they may be easier to find. For example: the Unitarian Church, which hosted the traveling canvas labyrinth twenty-five years ago, now has a permanent one paved on the grounds beneath a beloved oak tree. Another was recently placed nearby as a walking memorial to the forty-nine sacred souls we lost in the horrific Pulse nightclub shooting. Each name, never to be forgotten as we are encircled by their love, is illuminated by the light we send back to them.

One of the ways that I like to use this tool is for manifestation. Into the labyrinth, I carry my fears, my sorrows, my sense of the barriers that hold me back. Then, out of the labyrinth, I lift the vision of a new path forward, free from such obstacles and limiting belief.

I journey inward, consider what I need to release, and when I reach the center, I offer my gratitude for where I have been that delivered me to this moment of awareness. I give thanks for the hardship, which showed me my strength, and for the goodness that shall manifest for the blessing of my fortitude.

From that central focus on gratitude, I choose to leave behind that which no longer serves me, and return to the path unhindered. As I walk out on the same path that brought me here, I am lighter and open to receiving. I envision a future that brings new joy and different lessons that will further my evolution. Knowing that the path inward was unknown but safe, I can venture out with that knowledge. Wherever this path leads, I am safe, I am grateful, and I am never alone.

Another way that I have used the labyrinth was for a sort of past life regression. My soul-daughter is a medium. Earlier this year, she revealed to me a piece of a past life with my father. She offered me a morsel of that distant lifetime, which might reveal a deeper message for the one we now share. Her instruction was to meditate on it to see if healing could be found.

That weekend, I went away for a workshop on voice and sound healing and there I found on the grounds — a replica of the labyrinth from Chartres Cathedral. See what I mean about that indelible mark? Once again, the path falls back on itself and we are carried, once more, past where we have already been.

So, once again, I stepped onto that familiar path. This time, I carried the seeds of a story and as I walked, a vision was revealed to me. It was a lifetime of loss, sacrifice, blame, and regret. I don't consider myself to be all that creative or clever when it comes to writing fiction, so the unfolding of this story felt very real to me. A father and daughter who survived a natural disaster and the survivors' guilt that followed. The father had rescued the daughter, but failed to save others. She blamed him for his failure, but never considered that it was not for his fear of dying but for the unwillingness to leave her alone. She was his priority.

What did I carry out with me? In this lifetime, I can see that my father may not have rescued me from certain personal disaster (not that any have been so great), but that he has never left me alone. When my heart was first broken, he sat at my bedside and shed tears as he shared his loss of love when his sister died of cancer at forty. When my mom and I had issues in our relationship, he helped me to understand the wounds from her childhood, enabling me to love her more through the struggle, finding compassion, understanding, and forgiveness.

At this moment, my father is in the hospital. At age eighty-one, he has had a few struggles with his health and now he is dealing with an infection for which we are still awaiting illumination. I called him to let him know that I needed to finish writing this piece but that I would be there to see him soon. He assured me that he would be fine and that I didn't have to rush. What I know for sure is that I may not be able to rescue him from the natural disaster of aging, but I will be sure that he never feels alone.

When I sat down to write today, I had no idea that this path would lead me back to where I am right now. Like the sacred geometry of the labyrinth, I hoped to share with you the beauty that was revealed to me only when I came back around to this particular place on the path. Each time I come this way, I can see it from a new perspective and with greater insight. This is how the metaphor for life is mirrored.

So, if you have the opportunity to step into the welcoming embrace of a labyrinth, be it on a church floor or in a field of flowers—made of canvas and paint, or water-smoothed river rock—I hope that you will accept the challenge to go within. Spiraling in, carry your worries to be honored and left behind; spiraling out, be lifted by light and hope. There is so much beauty that surrounds you. All you have to do to find it is stop for a moment and look up.

Thank you for walking this sacred path with me. I just looked up to see you, and I am so glad you are here.

The Long and Winding Road – October 2018

This week, I am once again in the heart of the landscape that I love most, The Blue Ridge Mountains. Were it not for the cold, I could live here. For some, the ocean sings a song that calls them home, and for me it is the mountains. Not just any mountains, though. These rich, ancient, and wise mountains that paint a picture of Mother Earth in repose.

A dear friend has a family home here and when she learned that I was in retirement rehearsal, she invited me to join her for the annual fall family week in heaven. Their home has been in the family for generations and has such great history and energy; it is always an honor to be invited. A great deal of the adventure is just about sitting on the porch to breathe in the soothing sight of it all.

I've come home this evening from a trip to a nearby mountain town to find the house abandoned, and I am alone with the fire and the sound of wind in the trees outside. If I didn't know better, I might imagine that it is the soothing sound of ocean waves that shatters the silence and permeates the darkness beyond the living room windows. Looking up, I can see the luminous moon peeking in at me, as if to say, "What'cha writing, Missy?"

Yesterday and today brought even more delight, as I was able to visit with other friends who have homes on nearby mountains. There is a common theme in this connectedness. Each reunion provided the opportunity to go deep, to speak the truths of our individual journeys through challenges and into the gentle coming of peace.

It turns out that I am not the only one who has been presented with the opportunity to transform a way of life without clarity of outcome. Each of us were gifted the opportunity of presence for aging parents. Each of us have had to learn how to exist in a world vastly different from our former realities. Each of us have chosen a simpler life over the stressful intensity of that which we have left behind.

My friends have each experienced the mystery of divine timing and the way that all things wonderful managed to fall into place in the very best way, to enable the glory of prosperity, joy, and happiness. Though I feel as if I am not quite there, I have chosen to release fear and trust that this glory shall one day soon be mine, as well.

The road from one mountain home to another was a long and winding path of beauty and contemplation. Upon arrival, I shared with my friends how much the drive reminded me of walking the labyrinth. Focus and intention is required to keep your feet (or tires) firmly planted upon the path. If you are mindful, you can carry a problem, or concern, into the maze and carry out inspiration or a solution.

On this particular drive, I contemplated the way that this landscape fills my chest with a sense of wonder and delight. As leaves tumbled into the roadway, I held my breath until I was sure it was not a chipmunk crossing, grateful that I wouldn't have to swerve off the road and over the edge of a cliff. I was overcome with the blessings of nurturing and maintaining friendships with remarkable people in my life, whom I adore but have only "seen" on Facebook in recent years. And for that matter, considering the blessing of social media, which alerted these friends that I was heading their way This led to the greater blessing of invitations to reconnect and reflect.

The wind is picking up outside, and the roaring waves of tree leaves are crashing against the mountaintop as I reflect on our parting. With full bellies and grateful hearts, we reflected on how wonderful it was to be able to fall into togetherness, as if no time has passed, and to look forward to when we shall make it happen again. I love the way that community can mean so much more than those living in our immediate surroundings. I am thankful for the breadth of my community of generous and caring souls, which wraps around the Earth and grows larger with the reach of my writing. Seriously, I have the very best people!

Each night after dinner, the intention was to be on the road before nightfall to escape the probability of driving those winding roads in the dark. But each time, the company was so wonderful and too difficult to leave. I found myself witness to the retreat of sunlight through the trees as the road fell into darkness. And it brought me, once again, to the image that my soul-daughter painted to describe my present and my future.

I am on a dark road, and my car is safe with a full tank of gas. My GPS is guiding the way, but I can only see what is illuminated in my headlights. I know that I will reach my destination in divine timing, but all I can do for now is exactly what I am doing; keep driving, pay attention to what comes to light, and enjoy the beauty I find along the way.

As I contemplated this reality and this symbolism, the Universe did that thing it does that I love the most. It spoke to me through music. As I followed the darkened road, both literally and metaphorically, Stevie Nicks serenaded me with these words from her song, "Lady."

> And the time keeps going on by
> And I wonder what is to become of me
> And I'm unsure, I can't see my way
> And he says, "Lady, you don't need to see"

I am enormously happy to be in this car, on this dark road, guided divinely by the light of love. I'm unsure of where I'm going, but certain that I will know when I arrive. But more than anything, I am so thankful that you are here with me and I hope that you might also enjoy the drive.

Calling All Souls – October 2018

This morning, I rise with the company of thousands. On the Celtic holy day of *Samhain* (pronounced Sow-wen), their essence is nearer than any other day of the year. This year, I feel them in a way that was previously not possible. My intuitive gifts are not developed in a way that enables direct communication with those on the other side of the veil, yet . . . I know they are there.

My known ancestors will arrive today from across the pond. They hail from England, with a long-ago arrival on these shores via the Mayflower. They come from Scotland, as one of the four Marys who attended Mary, Queen of Scots. And they come from Ireland, which could explain why I cannot sit still through the waves of sound and percussion of Riverdance (seriously, I think there is something wrong with those who can).

I can see them all in my mind's eye, and they circle up around me, holding hands. From the center of their love, I walk among them to make eye contact and place my hand upon each of their hearts. Their love brought me here, and on this day I am grateful to offer mine in return.

Among the great loves of this circle are people who lived through hardship, and others who died in oppression (it is possible that some of my ancestors oppressed some of my other ancestors). But each had the courage to love. Some of them wished for a safer life, and departed the lands of their birth to seek something better; a life of freedom.

As the US midterm election is less than a week from *Samhain*, I am connecting with the wisdom and strength of those who have gone before me to ask that this circle of love and light illuminate this tradition to secure all that is right and true. Let all deception be revealed and brought to justice with haste.

By the strength and courage of every woman who has lived before me, and was involuntarily pushed into a life she would not have chosen for herself—but was forced on her by the patriarchy—and those who would keep her small for fear of the goddess given power she possessed, I ask that this be the election that turns the tides to bring greater balance into the stewardship of this great country. Let these women, who seek to nurture democracy, become like respected tribe mothers who serve beside men with hearts that are pure and not soiled by greed.

As we move into the dark part of the year, let a torch be lit that will be a beacon of hope that leads us back into the light.

Further, I ask for their protection. Of those who were once oppressed, I ask them to stand among those who are now oppressed to create a veil of safekeeping. It matters not the color of our skin or the spirituality of our hearts; we are all one and the same. Let us not be separated by fear and misunderstanding. Keep them safe. Keep us safe. Keep the US safe. Keep the world safe. Keep Mother Earth safe.

If this dark moment in our history is to be a lesson in fear, hatred, and greed that mirrors the past mistakes of other great nations, let us rise now to change the possible future from one that becomes yet another dark mark of shame on a land that was stolen at gunpoint from those who truly belong.

If our many wrongs can ever be made right, let this land be washed by a tsunami of love that tears down the walls that separate us so that our reach touches the hearts and hands of others rather than barbed wire and bullets.

Beloved Ancestors, of lines known and unknown that go back to the very beginning of time, know that you are honored on this day. For every hurt you suffered, I offer healing. For every injustice you endured, I offer compassion. For all of the love you shared, I offer more love.

For those I've lost whose names I have known: Ruth and Dan, Bill and Lil, Beth and Don, Gregg and Richard, Kirby, Ken, and most recently, Lynn, know that you are not forgotten. Today, my candle burns in your memory. Not in sorrow, but in joy. How blessed we all have been to get to walk this earthly plane at the same time.

Finally, for those who are reading these words . . . my candle also burns for those you have loved and lost. May you feel your beloveds coming ever closer on this sacred night and find comfort in sweet memories, and release for old sorrows. Our loved ones are safe on the other side of the veil, and their only desire remaining in the realm of the living is to be witness to our joy.

So, let's get to it! Create more joy. They left us early to remind us that time is fleeting. We wouldn't want them to think we missed the point.

Thank you for walking this sacred path with me. May your blessings be bountiful in this year's final harvest. Happy New Year!

Ode to Sanctuary – January 2019

My sweet Pop is back in the hospital. Year eighty-one has been pretty rough for him, and he is not even halfway through it. It's hard to see beyond this day-to-day mire when the truth is that it really won't get much easier.

Friends ask me what I am doing for self-care, as my entire world revolves around assisting my parents and friends facing serious health issues these days. Since I am experimenting with early retirement and an income a quarter of what it once was, the truth is that self-care, at the moment, looks like sitting at home alone.

So yesterday, I came home from the hospital and crashed hard in the embrace of the couch I bought when Arthur died. A traumatic loss, the cat who looked at me with such adoration—like no human I've known—dead within two hours of sneaking past me at the mailbox check. If you are gone, never to claw my furniture again, I'll show you; I'll get a new couch. But, oh, to yell at you to stop once more.

I slept on the couch for at least an hour, certain that I had become a stone memorial in repose from a Gorgon's glance. When I woke, I turned on the telly for background noise, and picked up my journal. More often than not, this is my journal, but my soul-daughter gave me a new book for Yule and it called to me.

Netflix showcased a season of *Tidying Up* with Marie Kondo. She started each session by greeting the house, and asked the inhabitants of each home to reflect on gratitude; thanking the house for its shelter, and to consider how they see their home in the future. So, guess what I wrote about.

I wrote a love letter to my house - my conduit of self-care.

Dear, beloved, gracious home:

Thank you for the protective shelter you have been for me these many years, and for the many years ahead.

I love the way you hold sacred memories of my personal history. I see, as I glance toward the kitchen, Nanny placing a chair at the sink, so I could help her wash dishes. I see granddaddy serving me a bowl of crumbled Graham crackers with milk at the dining room table.

In my mind's eye, I can see the place in the hall where the wooden cabinet that granddaddy built held the green rotary dial telephone with the long spiral cord (I can still hear it ring—delivering voices no longer heard upon the earth). In the library, I recall the mural on the wall that always reminded me of the hunting scene in Lucille Ball's movie *Mame*. And I remember Nanny, in the hospital bed holding her hand as it hung in the air—my final memory of her in this lifetime. Her spirit remains in this space and in the kitchen as well.

I see the faces of family and friends who have gathered here for more than twenty years (or fifty years, if we count those before

I made you my own). I honor once more every guest who has stayed, tribe rituals that altered our lives, and connection with the divine. Laurel dances from the hall into the living room, Rabbit prepares us a meal in the kitchen, Star Jasmine pours us a glass of wine. So many sacred circles in this space have turned it into a vortex of tangible magick. People comment on this feeling as they enter, and I just smile with a nod to the ether.

This home has given me peace, comfort, happiness, and joy. Every departure leaves me longing for return as I enter and walk into a hug. (An acknowledgment of your warmth from our friend, Joe.)

Oh, and the beloved pets who blessed my life, kept safe in your embrace . . . I love that they are all four still here, only one in corporeal form.

For our shared life to come, I thank you for sheltering and nurturing a loving, caring, healthy, reciprocal relationship for myself and the responsible, committed being who enters my life and pursues my heart with laughter and grace, then stays. Nanny smiles upon us, witnessing the long-awaited love that we have all dreamed of but had not previously found.

This love, for both of us, has been truly worth the wait. It heals hearts and souls throughout our genetic line and for lifetimes to come. This partnership brings freedom and prosperity and this home is nurtured and caressed in new and loving ways—making room and extending time for even more love to grow.

Thank you for all of this and for all that is yet to come, my beloved safe place and sanctuary. I love you so!

That last part is obviously just a dream of a possible future, but these things happen for others . . . why not for me? A recurring thought through these days of eldercare has been a longing for someone to comfort me, when I have spent my day comforting others. I love my life exactly as it is. If there is more for me than this, it will be a beautiful bonus that I am open to receive.

Thank you for walking this path with me. I can feel you here in my sacred space adding to the magick that resides within. Come by anytime and sit for a spell.

Take My Hand – January 2019

This morning I woke with an image of connectedness. With the awareness of our mutual suffering, and that of Mother Earth choking on the waste of our shortsightedness, I felt a yearning for us to move beyond this primal ache that resides somewhere between hearts and bellies and into the healing light of trans-formation.

There are days that I have checked the reach of my writing to discover that right here, within this sacred circle, are beautiful beings from all over the world. In truth, if you are reading these words—know that you are here beside me, held within this emerald green light of my heart's devotion. I am grateful for your presence in my life.

In this reading, if you feel safe and moved to do so, I wonder if you would imagine taking my hand into yours. If so, I would have us gather with every beloved heart that I know, that you know, and that those who have joined us here know, be they still upon the earth, or those who have passed into the mystery of what comes next. Let us stand within this circle, connected through hearts and hands, a circle so broad that it could encapsulate the world with the luminous light of love.

With the power of our togetherness, we elevate the vibration of the waves of energy that we cannot see with our eyes. The atmosphere that surrounds us has become muddled with so much oppression, fear, loathing, and unkindness that we can barely breathe. As we mingle our energy and hum a soothing *Om* into the atmosphere, the walls built by intolerance and self-hatred cannot withstand the reverberation of loving kindness. They come crumbling down.

If you are troubled or care for someone who is suffering, consider stepping into the center of this circle of human kindness to be filled with the light of love.

I carry this image in my heart of standing in the center of darkness, surrounded by those who love and support me without condition. There is firelight beyond them, which illuminates their profiles but keeps their faces in darkness. They remind me that though I stand in shadow, I am not alone.

As you imagine yourself standing in this shadow of winter's introspection, can you make out the silhouette of those who surround you? Can you sense their presence, their adoration, their love as it flows through you, surrounding you with the light of hope? Even if you are geographically distant, without a doubt you are still enveloped by their love.

Imagine, if you can, walking toward each sacred being and reaching out for their embrace. Spend some time here and consider who stands firmly within this circle. They may be members of your family, your tribe, or they could be loved ones who have passed beyond the veil. They may even be spirit guides and guardian angels (energetic beings of universal wisdom) whom you have never seen with the eyes, but whose presence has been evident. When you thought you were alone they arrived as you felt the warm glow of comfort and loving kindness.

Let each embrace be held at heart's center. Imagine chins over left shoulders as heartbeats come into unison, and knowledge is exchanged without words. When you have connected deeply with each sacred soul, choose a spot within the circle where you would like to stand and take the hands of those beside you.

As you make this palm-to-palm connection, a golden light begins to flow in a clockwise motion around the circle. This light expands to encase all who gather. But it doesn't stop here. It continues to grow like waves upon sand, slowly reaching further, leaving a glittering glow as it retreats and then surges beyond previous reach.

Witness the glowing expansion as it presents itself to loved ones who may also glory in the return of light. See their faces awash with radiance and reverence.

Let this light be carried into every dark corner of the earth and let every heart be healed. Love this light into ancient soil, to nourish and revitalize the Mother who gave birth to all life. This human experience is only made possible by her love.

Note: I was writing this yesterday, when my computer decided to take a break on me. As I toiled through troubleshooting on how to fix the issue with my brother (also PC support guy) three hours away, my phone rang. My mother was in the hospital following a car accident. Gratefully, she was relatively well, considering the appearance of her car, which was T-boned by a large truck, but we spent the rest of the evening in the ER running tests just to be sure. It was not lost on me that *she* is the mother who gave birth to my life and that *my* human experience was made possible by her love.

This, folks, is another one of those moments of gratitude in awareness. I am aware that the Universe conspired to set me free from the workplace in 2017, and enabled an early retirement income so that I could live simply and be fully present for my aging parents. As for this particular piece of writing . . . I have needed these virtual hugs more than anyone could possibly know.

The day before the accident, my mom and I set in motion the work necessary for me to handle financial matters on my parents' behalf, when the time comes that I can assist further with their care. As I sat in my own living room last night, having settled mom into hers, I reflected on how things might have gone differently . . . how our intentions might have missed their mark. I'm so grateful that, for today—having just heard her voice on the phone, informing me that she is awake and well—everything will be okay.

I hope that all is well with you and yours, also. Thank you for walking this path with me. I can see you bathed in golden light, and I'm so glad that you are here.

The Joy and the Sorrow – January 2019

If 2018, for me, was about *letting go* of my former self, the "me" I had been for twenty-five years in a career of supporting the wellness of two corporations, then 2019 will surely be about *becoming* the "me" of my future self.

Being officially retired and thrust into daily care for my parents has offered new freedom. As we face their struggles with body betrayal and memory loss, I have found the total immersion that has allowed my subconscious to sever the bonds that once tethered me to that former identity.

I no longer worry that I will have to return to that world or what it is that I should be doing with my time and energy. It seems that my time and energy, for this moment, is meant to serve my parents.

Full disclosure, as my fiftieth birthday approaches this weekend, there are times when I feel a little sad about where we are. I mean, I had once dreamed with childhood friends who also reach this milestone birthday in 2019, that we would make a celebratory trip to Greece or go back to Ireland together. But retirement living offers a different budget and being that far away for a length of time feels impossible.

But then . . . I come back to gratitude. I asked the Universe for prosperity that would allow freedom from the corporate world, and it provided an unexpected blessing (in the form of the IRS 72T loophole). I thought I would still need to work a full-time job (for less pay), but it turns out that I can live simply and have all I need on a quarter of my former income (for now).

I asked to be guided toward a meaningful purpose, and I thought I was led to becoming an end-of-life doula. Now, I'm not so sure that was for a path of prosperity as it was a path to peace. Spending a year studying death has brought me into a respectful relationship with what once was feared.

A doula is ultimately a transition/transformation guide—one who holds space for and supports those who are moving from one phase of life to another. A birth doula walks with the maiden as she becomes a mother and the death doula walks with the crone as she makes her way back to the mystery of what comes next.

I recently made the mistake of looking up the meaning of doula online, and the Greek origin of the word means "female slave." I am currently seeking a different word.

My family's new year is not off to a particularly joyful beginning. On New Year's Eve, I brought my eighty-one-year-old father back to the emergency room for an issue that has been ongoing since October. He was admitted, and then after a procedure, he went back to Rehab for strengthening his ability to stand and walk. Nine days later, my seventy-seven-year-old mother was T-boned by a careless driver while on her way to the store. So, back to the emergency room we went. Gratefully, major bruising was the extent of her injuries. Well, and serious emotional trauma, of course.

The fact that I am childless, single, and retired means that I have the freedom to be fully present for my parents. A lovely consequence is a deepening of our relationships with one another, a healing of old wounds, and a more patient and compassionate communication style. I feel that the three of us are learning and growing together in this period of transition. But to be clear . . . this is hard!

I am not really living for myself at the moment, but this is temporary. I have taken on multiple roles—sometimes nurse, sometimes accountant, manager, booking agent, driver, house-keeper, IT technician, etc. I am working as hard or harder than I did in the corporate world. Though I am not receiving a paycheck, feeling valued and appreciated by my parents feels like a much greater reward.

Somehow, the Universe will guide me to finding balance. I will learn about other resources to assist us on our journey, and I will learn how to surrender to the kindness of others. I will be available for the care of my parents, and I will not abandon myself and my own needs to a former belief that everyone else's comfort is more important than my own. I will continue to open to the mystery of receiving, which is not available to me, as long as I am always giving. I will meditate, take hot baths, and nap when I need to, because the energy that I give to others must be replenished. And somehow, I will create opportunities to do a little bit of living for me.

There is great sorrow in the obvious decline of our parents, and in the sense of loss of ourselves as we serve others. There is an overwhelming sense of aloneness (not always loneliness) at the end of the day, lying in bed awake with the worries of what lies ahead without a companion to remind, some of us (me) that everything will be okay.

But there is also great joy in the way that we are reminded that we are not walking alone in darkness. Those who love us are standing by, ready to shine in support of our path forward. They are here to give us a good squeeze when we feel that our guts might spill onto the earth below. There is incredible peace in realizing that everything we need is provided, falling into place with divine timing and often great surprise. There is enormous gratitude that things should be turning out exactly as they are, because this moment—in all of its darkness and light, trauma and recovery, solitude and unity—is somehow terribly and wonderfully perfect.

Thank you for walking this path with me, dear ones. I can feel you surround me and I hope that you can feel me in your circle, as well. I love you more.

What Is Your Joy? – February 2019

My friend Brian called from Oregon this morning. He wanted to thank me for the Valentines card I mailed last week. As we caught up on the details of the lives and loves of one another, he made a suggestion.

As I shared with him the workshops that I am creating to share a sense of mindful manifestation with others, he exclaimed, "You make such a difference in the lives of those who know you. You should share my story! I'll never forget what you asked me that night that we had dinner together, while my organs were literally shutting down." I almost lost my dear friend before he was able to answer this all-important question. If that alternate reality had come to pass, I wouldn't be who I am today. I never would have understood the magnitude of my great loss. In as many ways as I have blessed his life and brought about a more mindful existence . . . he has done the same for me.

Brian's courage to share his truth with me that day brought forth that morsel of wisdom that came through me. *Ask the question to help someone find their own solution.*

It has been a year since Brian made this declaration of joy, and it has been three months since he began pursuing his *joy* full time. Following our last conversation, he filed for disability from work, and went home to focus on his own wellness.

He shared today that his last check-up was pretty good. He feels good, and he is filling his days with more joy and less stress. This makes my heart so happy.

As for me, my joy is getting to connect deeply with others. That kind of surface connection just won't do. I want to know what makes your heart happy. I want to know what makes your soul sing. I want to know if you were given a terminal diagnosis tomorrow (heaven forbid), how you would choose to spend the rest of your days.

I was blessed to be able to take an early retirement of sorts, so that I can be present with the extra care that my parents need at this time in their lives. But as all caregivers should, I feel it necessary to find more balance in my life. Knowing that they are safe and well is gratifying, but there are days that are more difficult than others and I need to have something that fills my needs while I am filling theirs.

The workshops that I facilitate are a part of that plan. Together, my Sacred Gardeners and I planted our Seeds of Intention at Imbolc. As the wheel of the year turns and we greet the growing daylight in the Northern Hemisphere, we will celebrate the spring equinox. Twice a year, day and night are equal, and we are reminded that our needs are not unlike those of Mother Earth.

My second workshop is called, Persephone Rises: Finding Balance at the Equinox. Just the thought of it makes my heart push through dark, moist soil toward the expansion of the sun. We shall throw off our cloaks of winter and don the brilliance of springtime.

The intentions that we developed in February should start to take root, and it is up to us to ensure their freedom to grow.

I know that for me, finding balance means ensuring that I am creating ample opportunity to refill and recharge. Spending time with those I care about brings me joy, as does listening to live music—so I'll be having more of that. Also, I've dedicated to doing one of these workshops every eight weeks for the year, and even the planning brings me joy. Honoring Persephone as she emerges from the underworld makes me squeal with delight! But then . . . there will be the time spent with others who are willing and eager to seek something deeper for themselves and to become the joyful gardeners of their own lives. More than anything, I love to be witness to the growing glow of others.

So, tell me dear ones, *what is your joy*? I really want to know.

Thank you for walking this path with me. Your presence is also my joy.

Mindfully Human – February 2019

I am told that the reason we move out of energetic form into the human realm is so that we can have a "sensual" experience. In other words, we are here to learn and grow through the art of feeling.

Through my study of death, I have learned not to fear what comes next, as we will shift back into a different, less tangible form. This is a far cry from my childhood belief that we live, then die and simply cease to be.

Despite this shift in perspective, I still don't have a relationship with the concept of Heaven and Hell, as I am certain those are human constructs of manipulation (no offense). I tend to believe that those are possible realities right here on earth, depending on your circumstances and perception.

As I walked home from my parents' house last evening, feeling a mist of rain and wind upon my skin with the sensation of my heart filling at the sight of the Tabebuia tree in my neighbor's yard, which is in stunning full bloom the color of sunshine, I was overcome by the urgency of this experience.

It was as if the Universe was reminding me to drink it all in . . . every sensation and emotion, so that I will be able to carry them with me when my body ceases to house my soul.

As we leave the womb of our mother, we emerge into the light. As we grow, we are exposed to so many experiences that offer learning and growth to the consciousness of the soul and every lesson is deepened by touch, by sound, by taste, by sight, by smell, and by the words we share with one another.

On the other side of the veil, we continue to learn and grow, but it is very different in the absence of corporeal form. Imagine being educated about love without the tenderness of a caring caress. Imagine learning more about courage without feeling fear for the temporary nature of the body. Imagine trying to understand passion and desire without all of the elements that go into the experience of attainment. Imagine wrapping your love around someone without ever feeling their embrace.

There is so much here for us to learn, and it has nothing to do with marketable skills. If we are not placing value on the way the wind makes us feel as it runs wispy fingers through our hair, or how the gentle rain consecrates our sacred bodies with holy water from the sky above, or how the fire warms our skin and brings illumination to our camp songs and ghost stories, or how every inch of earth supports and nurtures our every footfall, we are horribly missing the point of this human experience.

Offering our love to others in the form of words or physical hugs is something that we can only do in human incarnation. When we flow back into the infinite energetic force of all that is, we will be nowhere and everywhere all at once. Sadly, our loved ones may not know it. Doesn't that make being here now of greater importance? Doesn't that make you want to go out and dance in the rain with anyone whose touch you will one day long to feel along the surface of your skin?

Textures, emotions, colors, the physical sensation of the elements of nature, tangible expressions of love, affection, and adoration . . . we cannot take these things with us. Allow your mind, body, and soul to drink in every sensual encounter as if it might be a hundred years before you have the chance to feel it again.

If we are mindful and present in every moment, there will be nothing to regret when we finally shed this mortal skin and rise into the freedom of what comes next. What a glorious thought! To know that we get to carry forth such luscious gratitude for every little thing.

Thank you for walking this path with me. I am enormously happy that you are here.

Check Your Treasure – April 2019

Yesterday was a day of service and recovery. My sweet eighty-one-year-old Pop had an early morning appointment to *finally* have the entropion on his left eye repaired. It developed one day while he was in rehab last November. I walked in for our nightly visit and he looked like he had pink-eye. But when I took a closer look, I could see that his eye lashes were rubbing against his cornea.

In my past life, I was paid to assist the needs of executives. It was stressful work at times, but there were perks, too. For one thing, if my executive wanted something done, I could reach out to others and say, "the Chief 'whatever' Officer, wants this done immediately!" And it would get done immediately. In my new life, there is very little power. I tell doctors, hospitals, rehab facilities, and so on that my eighty-one-year-old father needs something immediately, and after five months of suffering and struggle . . . we might be lucky enough to bring one nightmare to conclusion. It's maddening, really.

So, yesterday, though mornings are difficult for him, we were both up by 5:15 a.m. to get the day started. We had to report to the eye institute by 6:45 a.m. We were there thirty minutes early and were *not* going to let anything get in the way of getting this done. Since it started, he says that he feels like there is a fishnet hanging over his left eye. It impedes his vision and his balance. He didn't really need any help with the balance thing. He has neuropathy from toes to knees in both legs, and severe weakness on his entire left side from eighty years of epilepsy related nerve damage. WTF Universe? Don't you think he's had enough to deal with in this lifetime? Sheesh!

This morning, I was out of the house by 6:30 a.m. to make a run to the store for provisions. I walked into my parents' house and stocked the bathroom with my father's needs, put a few breakfast burritos in the freezer, refilled his water cup, placed an ice pack on his bruised and swollen eye, turned out the light, and slipped back out the door.

These moments of tenderness never cease to surprise me. I chose not to have children, and while I have loved my goddess babies deeply, it was never mine, to feel this particular sense of affection, patience, devotion, and care. Indeed, at times, supporting my father is like taking care of a child. He has tiny temper tantrums for the frustration of his body not cooperating with what his mind is asking. He grumbles under his breath about how my mother doesn't wear her hearing aids. Sometimes, I have to remind his inner grouch that it is not easy, for mom or for me, to do all that is required to keep him safe and at home. "So, be nice!"

But then there are the moments like this morning, or when I am helping him wash his hair or put on his socks with the grippy soles, and brushing the hair out of his eyes, I get an overwhelming sense that this must be how mothering feels. This must be the contented heart reason for all that mothers choose to endure.

It occurred to me the other day, that I won't stay in retirement forever. The workshops that I facilitate are enormously fulfilling, as they feed all five of my strengths (empathy, connectedness, responsibility, developer, input), they offer me a creative outlet in the design and execution, and they give me a place to put all of the spiritual growth and self-healing work I've done over the last twenty-seven years for the benefit of others. But at this moment, I can't see clearly how to mold this work into a financially sustaining endeavor. So, I believe that the Universe will deliver the guide, the means, the opportunity when the time is right. And for now, my priority remains the care and comfort of my parents with the added bonus of ample time for nurturing the love that resides within.

I couldn't be more grateful for all that has transpired in order to make all of this possible. I spoke to my friend Brian yesterday, while out on an errand to have Dad's glasses repaired. He called to check-in and to tell me that, despite his terminal diagnosis, he is doing well and living his joy. He is "Marie Kondo-ing" his home (much to his husband's chagrin), and practicing extreme self-care.

Getting to be fully present for my parents right now is my joy. Being blessed to have friends, old and new, join me on a journey of personal growth, healing, and development for a year-long series of workshops is my joy. Quality time with loved ones is my joy. Having the gift of words to share with you is my joy. Being awake and aware of the many synchronicities and blessings that fall before me daily is my joy.

I feel richer today than ever before. The relationships that bless my life are more valuable than gold and diamonds. I can see clearly that every one of these blessings are finite, and I shall not take a single one for granted.

This reminds me of the conversation that concluded my visit with my soul-daughter on Monday. She had come over from St. Petersburg for an appointment, and made time with me a priority. She had also connected with friends from a former workplace, but when it was time for her to meet with them there was no immediate reply. While I knew that I would always adjust my plans to include seeing people I care about, she was figuring out (at twenty-three) that she was not willing to sacrifice her precious time for those who do not make her a priority. At this young age, she has already figured out that she is meant to be treasured. I'll confess that it took me a bit longer.

It's never too late to check your treasure, dear ones. Take a look around you now. Who do you see? Remind yourself of the great bounty you possess. Then, go out there and live your joy! Thank you for walking this path with me. I'm so happy you are here.

An Early Harvest – June 2019

My favorite tomboy sent me a text yesterday, "I wanted you to know before you see it on Facebook…." I held my breath and read on; her nephew, the eldest son of her little brother, is dead.

She and I have been friends since she was four, and every interaction we share takes me back to that moment in kindergarten, when I made a lifelong friend. At the time, her brother was only three. I see him at that age, in my mind's eye, moving toy cars around an imaginary track on the floor, making sound effects through vibrating lips—and then jump ahead forty-five years to realize he will soon bury his twenty-eight-year-old son. We were preparing to comfort one another through lost parents—as each gathering brings news of obstacles or decline, but never . . . this.

I've been thinking about how I will add the topic of death into my workshops this year, but it is not slated until the end of summer, when symbolically, we prepare for the first harvest and the dance of the sacrificial king. This year, our harvest has come early. The sun is barely at its height. The fruit is on the limb but far from ripe. We are not ready. We are never ready.

I did not know him, this young man; gone too soon, but I understand that for many years of his youth, he walked in shadow. He wore the cloak of addiction, which kept him shrouded from his family's love until recently. He dropped the cloak through rehabilitation and recovery, and walked into the arms of his family. I know they will each hold this reunion in their hearts with gratitude as they grieve the loss of a son, a brother, a nephew, a cousin, a grandson . . . and the death of hope. Hope was something they held onto for a long time. The hope of peace and happiness for this beloved being. It may not have been a surprise a few years ago, but *this* was unexpected. Things had been going so well.

I studied death for a year, and I still struggle with knowing how to help. I am remaining connected to my favorite tomboy, ready to be of service to this family in which, I too, grew up—in a way. I am listening for her words of heartbreak (or rather—reading them via text, because speaking is just too difficult for her right now), and holding space for her sorrow. I know that I cannot make it better, but I can be present . . . and that is good enough.

I have pulled a few books from my little death library, and thumbed through the pages for the comfort I seek to provide. My lifelong friend is spiritual but not religious, and my resources are eclectic. From Starhawk's *Pagan Book of Living and Dying*, my favorite words of comfort are:

BLESSING OF THE ELEMENTS

May the air carry his spirit gently.
May the fire release his soul.
May the water wash him clean of pain and suffering.
May the earth receive him.
May the wheel turn again and bring him to rebirth.

The second book I reach for is *The Tibetan Book of Living and Dying* by Sogyal Rinpoche. There is so much wisdom here, but what draws me the most is the essential *phowa* practice. The practice is meant for those of us on a path of enlightenment to be prepared at the time of our death to be received beyond the veil. I am adapting the words provided in Practice One to symbolize our prayer on his behalf.

Through the blessing, grace, and guidance, through the power of the light that streams from the embodiment of truth:

May all of his negative karma, destructive emotions, obscurations, and blockages be purified and removed.

May he know himself forgiven for all the harm he may have thought and done.

May he accomplish this profound practice of *phowa*, and die a good and peaceful death, and through the triumph of his death, may he be able to benefit all other beings, living or dead.

May all who love this sacred being see him being illuminated and encased in this radiant light, as he is received with loving kindness by the embodiment of that which receives us and renews us.

May all stand witness to the cleansing and purification of his negative karma, destructive emotions, and all that may have caused his suffering or suffering to others.

May all see the light of his heart rise in rays of emerald green toward the golden light of compassion above him. As his soul feels the absence of all suffering with the gift of forgiveness, no longer held to the realm of regret, his being melts into light, and merges with the blissful presence.

May all find peace as he becomes one with all that is.

Finally, I love this piece from Megory Anderson's book *Sacred Dying: Creating Rituals for Embracing the End of Life*. It is attributed to an anonymous writer, found in *Life Prayers: From Around the World: 365 Prayers, Blessings, and Affirmations to Celebrate the Human Journey* by Elizabeth Roberts and Elias Amidon. I've seen it in social media in reference to Saying Kaddish, a Jewish tradition for the dead.

> When I die give what's left of me away to children and old men who wait to die. And if you need to weep, cry for your brother or sister walking the street beside you. And when you need me, put your arms around anyone and give them what you need to give me. I want to leave you something, something better than words or sounds. Look for me in the people I've known or loved. And if you cannot give me away, at least let me live in your eyes and not on your mind. You can love me best by letting hands touch hands, by letting bodies touch bodies, and by letting go of children that need to be free. Love doesn't die—people do. So when all that's left of me is love, give me away.

For this sacred family, and for that matter—for all who are suffering a loss that has come too soon, I hope that the good memories remain firmly rooted in the garden of their hearts, and that all sorrows, betrayals, regrets, and concerns unspoken are easily liberated from fertile soil, to be acknowledged, honored, and released—then tossed onto the burn pile to be transmuted and transformed into fertile new growth.

Sometimes, we can forge a stronger relationship with a soul that was too damaged to be reached in the mortal realm. May healing come to one and all, and in time . . . may sorrow give way to the gentle coming of peace.

I wish this story had a happier ending, and yet like all of us, the ending was the only guarantee from the beginning. I honor the story of this sacred soul—every difficult page and chapter, the triumph over addiction, and the final liberation. I rejoice in the freedom from oppression that now is his, especially that of his own mind. I stand witness to the melting of his body into the light of compassion, and know that he has found peace there. Amen. May it be so. Blessed be.

Witness to Waning – June 2019

I watch her from across the room and see her stumble. My kitty, Morgan, seems a bit wobbly this week, and I feel helpless. I pick her up and shower her with kisses, as I smooth out the water trapped in the fur of her forehead, spreading it into the fur of her neck and shoulders—an impromptu bath. I noticed this trend of dipping her head in the stream of water coming through the spout of her water fountain about the same time that the head tremor appeared. She is the fifth cat for whom I've had sole responsibility in my adult life, and I still crave the understanding of KSL (Kitty Sign Language).

The workshops that I am developing and sharing this year are based on the changing seasons and how, just like nature, we humans move through cycles in our lives. It is a practice in mindfulness to take notice of what is happening around us and what is happening within us. Using the garden metaphor, our year takes us from planting a seed, to sprouting and growth, to blossom and fruit, to harvest, and finally to rest before the cycle begins again.

Much like the seasons move through a rise and fall throughout the solar year, so does the moon through the lunar month.

In the life of a beloved pet (in my case, a sweet cat named Morgan), the new moon would welcome a suckling kitten—brand new and filled with sweetness and hope. The two weeks that fall between the new moon and the full moon are the waxing time of life, as they become feisty, playful, adventurous, curious, and a little destructive. When the moon is full, the cat is a healthy adult. This phase feels like it shines for a good long time, until one day . . . the light gradually begins to pour out of the cup of the moon. In the waning phase of moon and cat, things begin to change. They start to lose weight and you can feel the sharpness of bone through their fur. Health issues start to appear. Getting them to eat well is a struggle. And suddenly, you realize that you are only months, weeks, or days from dark moon.

The parallels in the health of my cats and the health of my father have been synchronistic. Gwydion was with me for thirteen years, and in his waning year, my father was suffering an undiagnosed B12 deficiency. Several trips to Mayo Clinic failed to recognize the elephant in the blood work, and by the time a local neurologist discovered it, permanent nerve damage was done. That was in 2008. That same year Gwydion developed cancer, and as we were seeing Dad grow stronger, I was preparing to let my boy go.

Now, in 2019 I see my kitty stumble and reflect on the state of my father's struggle to stand and walk without falling. Once again, the cup of the moon pours out Her light and I can feel darkness descending.

The lives of our pets are fleeting in comparison to our own lengthy stay upon planet Earth. So really, my father is in the waning part of the year . . . maybe late autumn, while Morgan is in the waning part of the moon, like the waning crescent. Somehow it helps, I think, to view our lives this way. A continuous cycle of change. I know each year with the emerging spring that winter will come again. (In Florida, that can be enormously comforting.)

With all of the reading I've done on death and dying, and with greater understanding of the way that energy and consciousness (that which we are beyond this earthly shell) moves through space and time, my approach to nurturing both Morgan and Dad is more mindful.

If either of them does not want to eat, I offer an alternative. If they refuse that option, I let them be. I will treat for comfort, but I will not put either of them through anything that will be traumatic with the intention of prolonging life. Great clarity was attained in my reading of Stephen Jenkinson's *Die Wise*, and the painful awareness of his palliative care patients who ultimately felt resentful for *prolonged dying*. His style is poetic and blunt, so it's not the easiest read, but it is honest and insightful.

Dad and Morgan can both be quite stubborn. Getting Morgan to take her medicine or eat her food is often a struggle while she is quite good at water consumption. I don't have to worry about dehydration, at least. Dad, on the other hand consumes very little liquid, because getting up to empty his bladder requires so much effort. At least I can easily get him to tip his head back while I dump a hand full of pills into his mouth. I remind him every once in a while, that dehydration means a hospital visit, but then I drop it.

Learning to have healthy boundaries means respecting the autonomy of others. My approach to caring for my waning beloveds is more about presence and holding space than fixing things. When it is time for each to go they will go. We are all meant to go at some point, after all. I can do nothing to stop them. What I can do is love them. I can love them when they are sweet, and I can love them when they are cranky. I can love them when they move easily to my will and good intentions, and I can love them through their resistance.

My personal practice of mindful presence is to do my best to take notice of changes, to ask for help if I need it, and to offer pathways toward comfort and peace. At least in Dad's case, I can ask him if something we are doing is helpful or bothersome. Most of the time he isn't really sure, but there is always comfort in knowing I am not making it worse.

With Morgan, it is harder. Bargaining with a cat is complicated, and the only way I can determine if something is helping is if her behavior changes. When she turns her nose up at the same food she ate with gusto yesterday, I don't know what has changed or how to make it better. There are days when I have five different kinds of food down for her and dump it all the next day, barely touched. I consult with her doctor periodically and I try each suggestion. At the end of the day, we don't seem to be making much of a difference. And so, I return to my practice and hold her close.

Imagining the beauty of the moon in the night sky, even at the noon hour, I love the way she makes me feel. She reflects the radiance of the sun and illuminates the darkness. I guess that's what our pets do for us, isn't it? They illuminate our personal darkness. They are bringers of light. They add beauty and magick to our lives like nothing else my mind can gather. Even when the moon is dark, I know that she is there and I can feel her pull my internal tides . . . just as I sit in the living room now, while Morgan is at the library window, I can feel her pulling my heart ever to her own. I will hate to see her go.

Even facing the inevitable, fifth great loss in twenty-seven years, I wouldn't change a thing. It turns out that it really is better to have loved and lost, than to have never loved at all.

When Morgan's brother died four years ago, our veterinarian sent us a card, sharing our grief. The quote within captures this feeling so well:

We who choose to surround ourselves with lives even more temporary than our own live within a fragile circle, easily and often breached. Unable to accept its awful gaps, we still would live no other way. We cherish memory as the only certain immortality, never fully understanding the necessary plan . . .

"The Once Again Prince," from *Separate Lifetimes* by Irving Townsend

Being of service has always been my joy. Getting to serve my most beloved beings throughout their waning phase of life is not only my joy, but also my privilege and great honor. Their immortality is assured in the radiant fullness of my cherished memories.

Thank you for walking this path with me.

The Weight of Grief – July 2019

Today, I feel heavy. I feel it in my chest, as if I must push out every breath. I feel it in my joints and fascia. Everything hurts today. Even my fingers hurt as I type.

There has been news this week of a friend who lost her husband suddenly and without warning. His departure is tragically similar to the loss suffered by another friend, who is painfully triggered by these events. At the same time that this news arrived, I learned that my former work partner's sixteen-year-old granddaughter has not been seen or heard from in four days (as of today). The presence of my sixteen-year-old grandniece, who is staying with me this week, brings this sense of fear and concern even closer to my awareness.

On top of this heartbreak is the continued witness of my father's physical decline. Only seven houses away, I got the call yesterday that he needed help. He had fallen on the way to the bathroom, and mom was able to get the Indeelift to him so that he could use the electronic device to bring him from the floor to a seated position, but he was not strong enough to stand from there and they needed help.

I helped him to the toilet and while he was there, we checked his blood pressure. It was surprisingly normal despite not having taken the prescribed pill to elevate his low blood pressure. We suspect it was due to the trauma and stress of the fall and effort to rise. His elbow was bleeding.

When we got him safely back into his recliner, I gave him a handful of pills from his morning pill box and fixed him a bagel and coffee. His head was hurting, so I encouraged consumption of caffeine to wait for the Acetaminophen to kick in.

My grandniece called from my house to be sure he was okay. She was worried that I'd been gone so long. When she arrived a week ago, she shared that she felt Dad was depressed because he didn't seem excited to see her. I told him about it later that night, when I went over to "tuck them in" (how I refer to being sure their doors are closed and locked, and everyone has what they need before bed), and he seemed to become more engaged with each of her visits. They taught themselves how to play poker via a YouTube video, and I think he rather enjoyed winning most of the foreign coins I had given them to use in lieu of poker chips. He beat her at several hands. We are going to miss her so much when she goes home.

My soul-daughter stopped by for a visit this morning, and this month marks the third anniversary of her boyfriend's death in a car accident. She was feeling anxious being back in town, where they had grown up together, and we spent some time talking about grief.

For me, when my father's soul decides to leave this earthly realm, I will experience my most significant loss. We discussed the importance of this time that he and I have together, to get to know one another in a more intimate way. It almost feels as if we have only known each other on the surface for the past fifty years. Now, we have dedicated time to understand the deeper truths within, even if not on a conscious level. Lately, it feels like I've been getting to know his stubborn and defiant inner child, and I love him just the same.

My intuitive soul-daughter tells me that what I feel right now, this ache for the unknown future, a sort of pre-grieving, will be the worst part. She feels that as things progress that I will find strength to be present and serve each situation with grace. This part of our story will be an important part of my becoming. I hope she's right about finding strength.

Sometimes I feel like crying but the tears won't come. I recognized the other day that I was feeling like I did when I was an executive assistant supporting my beloved boss through a very difficult time in our corporate history. I felt that I could not be away from the office, because it would be a hardship for her to feel unsupported. I had five weeks of vacation but would only take time off if she went away.

Dad has surgery scheduled for the end of July. I feel the need for a break, but am struggling with the idea of being an hour away, let alone the ten-hour distance at the place that fills me up. Yet, I know that I will be a better caregiver with that respite. Whatever his recovery may require, I will be stronger and healthier to be present for both of my parents if I make my own self-care a priority.

So, I am nervously making plans for a mini-vacation. I had planned to take my grandniece north to see the fireflies, but it seems the Universe is pushing me toward another solitary journey (she has to return home earlier than planned). I suspect introspection comes easier for me that way, and that's where I do my best work; it is an inside job.

I know that my parents will be fine while I'm gone. At least mom says they will be fine. Dad says, "Speak for yourself!" I'm afraid he won't take his pills each morning and night. I'm afraid he won't ask for what he needs. They are both forgetful, and I've arrived some evenings and asked what he had to eat, and both of them realized that he hadn't really had anything since breakfast.

I'm afraid he'll fall and they will have trouble getting him back to his feet. I'm afraid of the fear and loneliness he might feel in the moments he realizes that I am not answering his call for help . . . and now I have arrived at the core of where we are.

Harville Hendrix says that our core wound of abandonment comes from the first time we cry out for our parents from the crib, and our cry goes unanswered. At that stage, we need our parents for sheer survival, not to mention all of the other good stuff they provide. That's not to say that my dad needs me for his survival, but I certainly don't want him to ever feel abandoned. His body is betraying him at every turn and I don't plan to contribute to that turmoil, if at all possible.

This also reminds me of the month that I cared for my grandniece when she was eighteen months old. Her mother and grandparents had to be away, and she would cry if I left the room. I was painfully aware of the status of her feelings of abandonment, so I would carry her with me to the bathroom if she woke up before I'd had time for my morning tinkle. I would have done anything to keep her from feeling abandoned. Did I mention that empathy is my number one strength?

If I am to practice what I preach, I will be sure to care for the caregiver. One of the many blessings of friendship is that when we are in need, those who love us will rise to our service. One friend has offered a beautiful space for my escape, and another has offered to stay in my home while I'm away so that my parents may call and still have someone at the door within two minutes to offer support.

I have a candle lit as a beacon to bring my friend's grand-daughter safely home, and I am working on a ritual to support and nurture the transition of my friend's husband who has gone too soon. I know that they, too, are feeling the loving kindness of friends and loved ones who would do anything to make everything alright again, and I believe in the very best possible outcome for one and all.

An oracle card that crossed my screen today from *The Universe Has Your Back*, reads, "I find a deeper meaning and personal growth amid the discomfort." And boy do I feel uncomfortable right now. So many of us are suffering that it seems to be manifesting in tangible ways, be it body aches, troubled sleep, or a needed reminder to just breathe. Surely, we are being encouraged to offer more kindness to ourselves and others.

The other message that rose today was Layla from Alana Fairchild's Rumi Oracle. She informs us that in the darkness, there is the path. She urges us not to turn from it, but to sit with it, this lack of knowing. Anything about us that is untrue will be annihilated in this darkness. This darkness is essential for the appearance of the light that is on its way. She suggests that we welcome the darkness of our grief and suffering, and bear witness. We must allow the unfolding of the interplay of the darkness and the light for the enhancement of our own growth process, and here we shall also find joy.

Wouldn't it be nice if growth didn't have to hurt so much? If you find yourself walking through darkness right now, I hope that you know you are not alone. Take my hand, dear one. Together we shall bear witness to the darkness, and move forward into the light. Thank you for walking this path with me.

Caregiver Respite – July 2019

Yesterday, I drove eleven hours to reach my Nirvana. Before chosen as a somewhat popular band name, this was the transcendent state in which there is neither suffering, desire, nor sense of self—the final goal of Buddhism. In the symbolic sense, I find these things not at ocean's edge (only an hour from my home), but on mountain top. In the Blue Ridge Mountains, my soul finds peace, renewal, and rebirth.

My parents and I have fallen into such a lovely routine of presence and connectedness, that it was difficult to find the right timing for my absence but, as it often does, the Universe conspired for my highest good and everything fell into place. My friends with a bed-and-breakfast in Banner Elk, NC had one bed available, my brother planned a weekend visit with the folks, and suddenly my worries about abandoning my cat and my parents were lifted.

I once dreaded a long drive, even with a friend, for the tedious nature of the journey . . . trying to stay awake, stopping to pee in a public restroom, the way the body rebels from prolonged sitting/riding. But in recent years, I've learned to love such a journey, even solo. Yesterday, I enjoyed eleven hours of introspection.

I listened to an audiobook on spirituality, then needed more stimulation, so I sang along with the cast of *Hamilton*, and then spent some time with Alexander Hamilton's biography (also on audiobook), which informed Lin-Manuel Miranda's epic Broadway show. I found myself wishing there had been such art available in my youth, for learning about history would have been even more interesting to me if I could hum the tune.

I am grateful that I am able to find just as much joy in solitude as I do with great company. Maybe I have become the change I most wish to see in the world.

I arrived at my friends' home just before dinner time, after leaving home at 6:06 a.m. Oh, the glory of walking into open loving arms after a long drive. I was informed that four of the seven other guests were teachers, and one was a childhood friend of our hostess. They had grown up together and had gone all the way through school but had not seen each other in thirty years. This "business" has delivered the prosperity of reunion to my dear friend. The peace in her heart is tangible, and I am grateful.

After dinner, I learned more about the teacher-guests. They live near the DC area, and if you've ever seen video footage of the T-Rex protesting the president in front of the White House, well . . . you'll know that I have been blessed to meet a few remarkable and energetic beings who carry humor for protection during difficult times. It turns out that this group of friends drove down to attend the Scottish Highland Games on Grandfather Mountain. We learned that we share a common world view, spiritual path, and even world travel experience. We are kindred. It was difficult to turn down the invitation to join them for the games, but I reminded myself that I have come here to reconnect with the spirit that lives in the woods. Men in kilts will have to wait for another day.

I am sitting in a napping porch swing with my laptop, looking out at a mountain range, listening to the wind in the leaves and various bird call. I am bearing witness to bees and chipmunks in the yard. It is glorious. This is how my soul finds renewal . . . in the majesty of Mother Nature, in Her form of ancient, voluptuous, undulating mountain curves and folds. She allows me to sit in Her lap as She gently strokes my hair, and I am at peace. There are gray clouds above and I am hoping to add the sound of mountain rain to my weekend soundtrack.

On my drive, I was thinking about a sweet friend who is facing some health concerns. She has been having trouble sleeping lately, and reached out for support. On that road I drove, which sometimes presented obstacles, I started writing a meditation for her in my mind. What was to be a nine-and-a-half-hour drive (per Google maps) ended up being an eleven-hour journey. Most of the road was smooth and delightfully free-flowing. But once in a while there were obstacles. Some stops were just to empty my bladder and keep going, but then there was . . . South Carolina. It is the only stretch of I-95 I've driven that instantly changes at the border . . . shrinking down to two lanes in each direction. An accident that didn't even block the road cost all drivers an extra forty minutes as everyone slowed down to look, and there was nowhere for a non-nosy driver to pass.

When my friend was given a diagnosis and learned surgery was required, an obstacle was presented in the form of a heart concern. So, she has been momentarily diverted and things have slowed down to ensure she stays safe. But soon, the obstacle will be behind her and the road ahead will be free-flowing once again. She may need to stop for gas or to empty her bladder, but the road will patiently await her eager return to the path of discovery and freedom.

What a blessing it is that we all get to share our sacred journeys with the hearts of others. How lovely to seek healing and respite and to find it in the embrace of those we love. What wonder to be nourished and nurtured by a joyful welcome, deep sharing, caring inquiry, and in the honor of holding space for one another. In my heart, I know that *this* is the meaning of life. We are the Universe made manifest in human form for the delight of being touched.

I look up to see two souls at play, a small bird and a chipmunk at the edge of the yard. What a shame it would be to be in the presence of such grace and miss the point.

For the moment, I am comforted to know that my most important beings are caring for one another back home while I am doing the necessary work of caring for the caregiver (that's me). When I get home, we will get Dad ready for a surgery that will hopefully bring comfort, but will also require closer care through recovery. I am recharging my battery and will be ready to serve with presence, patience, reverence, and grace (so mote it be).

I'm planning to close this sacred writing tool and relax on the napping swing for a while. The meditation for my friend, to help her rest, will solidify in my mind to be written and recorded, and later, my hosts and I will ride down the mountain to share a meal. We are all eager to hear the Highland Tales of my fellow guests around the fire this evening. Until then . . . *Slainte*! (Gaelic, "To Your Good Health!")

Thank you for walking this path with me. I'm so happy you are here.

Fruition Unfolding – July 2019

Yesterday was one of those days that felt like a mixed blessing. It was spent in service to the health of my father. There were parts that were difficult for both of us, but throughout each moment, I was aware of my gratitude.

It started with a trip to Longwood to exchange his broken CPAP machine, then back to help him with his bath—washing his hair and scrubbing his scalp. Helping him dress, giving him his meds with a bottle of Ensure, feeding him a late breakfast with strong coffee, then getting him safely into the car and off to the hospital for an afternoon of testing.

If I were still in the corporate world, my Friday in service to my father would have been taken as a personal day or an accrued vacation day. I would have been moving through each task with thoughts of what I would have to make up for at work on Monday, for having been absent today. I am certain that such awareness would have made me less present in caring for my father. So . . . even through the parts where he and I had to struggle through a task, for his body betrayal requires assistance for tasks that might be simple for others, I was mindfully happy to be there in the struggle with him.

I wish that my father, at nearly eighty-two, could have the strength and dexterity to provide a simple urine sample to prepare for next week's urethral stricture repair (a four-hour surgery), but getting up from the wheelchair and onto a toilet seat in a restroom that lacks enough room and support bars in the right places is tedious. So, collecting a simple urine sample requires strength, compassion, and patience.

He is frustrated by the limitations of his body, burdened by severe bilateral neuropathy after a lifetime with epilepsy, and muscle loss. All I can do is offer my assistance and let him know that I am sorry for his struggle, and how I wish I could make it easier for him.

By the time we got home from the pre-surgery appointment at the hospital, we were both exhausted. I got him settled into his recliner, and went home for some light reading and a nap.

I read an article that my mother posted about death and dying, and I shared it with my workshop attendees. On August 3, we will honor the cycle of seasons at the Celtic calendar's first harvest, a cross quarter holiday referred to as *Lammas* or *Lughnasadh*. We will begin the discussion of death, but not in the sense of sorrow as death is as much a part of life as eating and sleeping. My plan is to help us find comfort in preparedness, for when we carry an umbrella it is less likely to rain. So, if we have a departure plan ready, all that is left for us to do is to live fully in the *now*.

I was already familiar with this *Die Well* ritual, as it was written in my required reading for a course on end-of-life doula I started last year.

Another article I read was my own blog post from this time last year, called "Homecoming." Last summer, I was more at ease about being away for a couple of weeks, and this post was about my return from the mountains. This year, four nights away felt risky and selfish, but it also felt necessary to offer my soul respite.

As I read what I had written, I realized that much of the uncertainty that I was experiencing at that time, and the hopes that I offered up to the Universe, had actually manifested over the last year, with grace and ease. And here's the thing . . . none of it was within my imagining. I resolved to allow the Universe to surprise me—and that, She did.

In fact, reading that post inspired me to walk over to my parents' house to "tuck them in" for the night. As I stepped off my sidewalk and onto the rain dampened street, I looked into the darkened sky to see one of our neighborhood bats fluttering about for an evening snack. I always feel blessed by a bat sighting. When one lives in the city, connecting with nature can feel like a rare opportunity.

When I entered my folks' home, Mom paused the movie she was watching and rewound a scene and asked me to watch. The movie was *The Bad Mother*, and a daughter was reading to her comatose mother from her journal. She read off a list of resentments for a multitude of wrongs she felt her mother had done to her in her youth. Then, my mom paused the scene and asked me if the things this character expressed to her mother were things I felt toward her, my own mother. She felt sure that I had every right to feel many of the things spoken (except for the hitting part—that was not a part of our shared story, thankfully).

As I paused to reflect, not only on the scene, but on my life and childhood, and also on the articles I read before coming over—I was taken by mindful awareness of the gift of this very moment. I acknowledged certain experiences that left wounds and resulted in false self-belief, but I also shared the discoveries made in my own personal development and healing. The knowledge that she had poor parental role models for her own mothering. Understanding that some of the wounds I received were wounds she carried from her own childhood.

Then, she said, "I'm so sorry for all of the things I did that harmed you." And I assured her that I let go of resentment long ago, and also, that I forgive her. I asked her for forgiveness for the things that I have done that hurt her, as well. She said that she forgives me, too. And then . . . she showed me a photograph of a hairstyle that she's considering with her next haircut.

I made sure that the doors of my parents' home were shut and locked, and that my canine siblings were well loved. I made sure that Dad had all he needed for the night, and told everyone that I would see them tomorrow. I walked home with happy tears leaking from my eyes, and great peace in my heart. I realize that for my parents and myself, all that is left for us to do is to live as fully as our earthly bodies allow. All is right with our souls.

This morning, Dad used Alexa to call me for assistance. Mom was asleep and is hearing impaired, so she couldn't hear his call. I helped him up off the floor with mechanical assistance (IndeeLift is one of many purchases we've made in the past year to enable better living for my father), got him settled into his chair, and served him a bagel and coffee. A new day of being of service has begun.

I can use my words from this time last year to conclude this post, with only slight adjustments—though I am no longer in the mountains, I am still surrounded by overwhelming grace and beauty. I am not fearful of the future and I know that divine timing will allow all that is needed to fall into place exactly as it should (much already has, and I am open to whatever awaits), and for all of this, and I mean all of it (including that which divine timing will later allow), I am eternally grateful. Thank you for walking this path with me.

First Harvest – Lammastide Rite – August 2019

On Saturday, I led my fifth workshop in a series of eight. It was the progression of Seeds of Intention planted in February. I'm making them up as I go, but they are inspired by the cycle of the sun and ever-changing seasons marked by the calendar of the ancient Celts.

The beginning of August marks the halfway point between the summer solstice (the longest day) and the autumn equinox (when day and night are equal). In farming cultures, this was when certain seeds (like wheat and corn) we planted at *Imbolc* (im-blk), in February, had grown to fruition and were ready for scythe and bundle.

It is from this tradition the song John Barleycorn was originally sung, which tells of a symbolic sacrificial king. We harvest mostly to sustain us through the coming winter, but some must be returned to the land to ensure next year's harvest and survival.

This reminds me of how we, as caregivers, simply cannot give every bit of ourselves to others. We must hold back something that remains ours alone. If we give it all away, whatever will we grow next year? How can we bake bread to nourish ourselves, if we have already offered every grain for the benefit of others?

Since I spent last year studying death and dying, this felt like the perfect timing to begin the discussion of death. My goal was not to dive into fear and sorrow, but to overcome it.

The one guarantee we are given at birth is that we will also die. Yet, many of us fear that eventuality to the point of denial. Loved ones pass with or without warning having never discussed the topic of inevitability. And those who remain are left in their greatest moments of shock and sorrow to guess what those they held sacred might have wanted to occur when their bodies were left behind and their light returned to the collective. So, I shared with my Sacred

Gardeners (my workshop attendees) the story of my friend Brian to inspire the day's task.

Since I like to offer a meditation or grounding technique at the start of each workshop, I chose to share a meditation I wrote to be a part of my own farewell ritual to be performed when I am gone.

In the visualization, I ask those who are mourning my loss to offer me their burdens, that I might take them away with me—so that they no longer need to carry such heaviness. And when they opened their eyes (and some wiped away tears) I asked them to write those burdens down and drop them into a "box of surrender" that I had previously crafted

Each of us spoke these words, "I surrender this burden to the light of love. I know that all is well in this moment. I trust that all shall be revealed in divine timing. "

Those burdens will stay in the box until we burn them at the winter solstice, but I can imagine from the words of introduction shared by each as the workshop began, that we are all carrying heaviness in our hearts that no one can imagine at a glance.

Next, I handed out copies of the Florida approved form for Advance Directive, a handbook on making end of life decisions, and a sample of the Five Wishes document, which offers suggestions that are helpful when one cannot imagine their own end of days.

We talked about what is important to consider, and about what we've experienced through the loss of those we have loved. We found comfort in knowing that when we carry an umbrella, it rarely rains. And so, we understand that once we have done the work to prepare for our peaceful ending, we have nothing left to do but to be like Brian and live more fully in our own joy.

After lunch, and after sharing the deep discussion of death and dying and preparedness, we moved into the creative/artistic portion of our gathering. Everyone decorated and dedicated their own boxes of surrender. Tosha Silver refers to this in her book *Outrageous Openness*, as a "God Box." Instead of carrying the burden of a probable future, she offers us a liberating tool for release. Some would say, "Let go and let God," but some of us are less comfortable with the term, and so we offer our hopes and fears to the light of love.

I provided wooden boxes, already primed, with paint, glue, glitter, and various bits and gems so that each Gardener could put into this "intention" their own creative energy. Let me tell you, they are works of pure beauty. When they open the lid to enter their handwritten worries, they are greeted by the words, "Surrender to Love," and "Resolved for the Highest Good in Divine Timing."

My hope is that my beloveds will acknowledge what weighs heavy on their hearts, honor them, and then lay them down with the knowledge and belief that all is well in this moment, which is all we really have. This leaves them time to rest in the belief that everything will be okay (even when answers don't arrive on our preferred timetable).

It was a long and wonderful day. I stopped in to check on my parents and Mom informed me of a mass shooting reported Saturday evening. On Sunday morning, when I went over to set them up for the day, Mom said, "Melissa, there was *another* mass shooting." At first, I thought she might have forgotten she had already told me. But then it sunk in. Two mass shootings in one twenty-four hour period. Another harvest. Another sacrificial king. Another tragedy to build on so many others, for which nothing has been done beyond inciting more of the same.

My book group met Sunday afternoon. We discussed how thrilled we were that though we read another book about slavery, it turned out to surprise us with the uplifting courage of two sisters who lived in Charleston, SC in the 1800s. Sue Monk Kidd's *The Invention of Wings* absolutely *wowed* us the way that her first novel, *The Secret Life of Bees* had done many years before.

My friend and coworker invited me into her book group about sixteen years ago to add diversity. So, as the only white girl in the circle, I had to bring up my curiosity for how my dear friends were feeling. My only burden is that of white privilege, and I feel overwhelmed by the blatant racism that is spewed, celebrated, and even protected by the GOP. I can only imagine how my friends might be feeling, and so I inquired.

My friend, who is black and grew up in Barbados, it turns out, does not carry the weight of discrimination as one might expect, though she could tell a story of living in NYC and having a frequent caller stop calling after meeting her in person to discover the color of her skin. And my friend, who is of Indian descent and grew up in England, remembers a child calling her family names as they exited a tour bus, but acknowledges that someone silenced the kid and they went on about their day. But we all cried as our friend, who is Latina and whose husband is black, told us of how she and her husband cried at the news of the latest massacre, and the manifesto that was revealed by the white nationalist terrorist before his shooting spree. We cried with her for the awareness that she and her beloved would be a target of such senseless violence. We cried for those who *were* the target of such hatred. We cried for all that feels lost to us in our beloved country.

After my book group selected the next book and put a date on the calendar, I hugged each a little tighter. Then at bedtime, I wrote onto a piece of paper: Keep Them Safe, Stop the Violence, Deliver Peace, Comfort Fear. As I placed it into my own Box of Surrender, I said these words, "I surrender this burden to the light of love. I know that all is well in this moment. I trust that all shall be revealed in divine timing. Please let it be soon."

Thank you for walking this path with me. Now, hand me your burdens and let them go. I will carry them away with me into the light of love.

Witness to Grace – August 2019
A High King Ascends to the Summerland

It was forty-five years ago that my favorite tomboy entered my life. She brought with her a lifetime of creativity, play, laughter, joy, and sharing. She has shared many vacations with me, of course many memories, and significant to this tale, she has shared with me her beloved family.

On Thursday, my lifelong friend and I hopped on a plane to Huntsville, Alabama. I don't believe either of us, while envisioning which path to take on our annual art-cation adventures, would have chosen this particular place as a destination (two progressive feminists went to Alabama), but after this past weekend, I can assure you that it will be a part of future road trips.

Nearly a decade ago, my buddy introduced me to her cousin through Facebook. Their mothers are sisters, but they did not grow up together, so it was a family reunion that brought them together as adults. And through connecting online about family heritage and sharing memories, they found like-minds in one another. Further, my friend could see in her cousin, a bit of me.

It's funny how we are able to connect through writing and sharing on social media to find something much deeper than words and photos. Somehow, if we are lucky, we manage to find communion. Not one person I met over the past four days felt like a stranger to me.

The reason for our journey North was one of pilgrimage. We arrived with open hearts and serving hands to honor the memory of a soul who departed around this time last year. Once again, he was a man that neither of us had the pleasure to have met in person, but through this sharing medium and from the heart of this lady that we love, he became legend.

Our kindred spirits were partially connected through common ground, a spiritual path, a world view, a love of ancient history and myth, and for the Emerald Isle where we had both previously traveled. Connected by the web of life and the world wide web, we shared photos and our stories. Then one day, the story took a dark turn. Her husband suffered a life altering spinal injury in a car accident, and the lives of many would be dramatically affected through an epic journey of survival for the next seven years.

Being so far away, the best that my lifelong friend and I could do was hold space and send the light of love, healing energy, and our desire for the very best possible outcome for this gentle giant and those he loved. And when his earthly body was ready to surrender his larger-than-life soul into the light of truth, we committed to being fully present to offer support and to celebrate his life. After much needed rest and recovery, and with the nearing first anniversary of his loss, it was time.

Looking back on the weekend I just left behind, it seems funny to consider how we walked into this woman's world and felt immediately at home. Though they are cousins, my favorite tomboy only has memory of meeting in person this daughter of her mother's sister once. Any previous meeting would have been at an age before memories were kept.

Since I have had front row seats in her life, those we met and the lives they discussed felt inclusive and familiar. After all, I had partially grown up in her home with her people, too. Amidst the connectedness, the laughter, and the enlightenment (as blank pages in family awareness were filled), we prepared for the celebration to come.

Last year, as I studied the path of end-of-life doula, I was instructed to consider this part of dying, how do I wish to be remembered? If I were to write my own memorial service, what would that look like? I have to tell you, these people . . . they know how to throw a party! I may write an addendum to my own parting plan.

As our hostess went to the airport to fetch her sister, my buddy and I were given the task of putting together one facet of the table decorations. We laughed at how perfect it was for us to receive this assignment. Lovers of Mother Earth, the party planners had collected earthen pottery and lichen laden sticks of oak for table center pieces. We delighted in examining each limb and cooed over the sweetness of tiny green tufts of fluff that called these fallen twigs home, "Look at this one! Aww . . . so cute. Which one do you think will go best with this taller stick? This one! No, *this* one." With smiles of agreement and sighs of adoration for these tiny bits of beauty, we gleefully completed our first task.

Later that night, we were given our second task. We went to the home of our dear one's best friend. We became acquainted around the same time as our initial Facebook connection, as a nod to those kindred details mentioned above. We were immediately smitten with our new/old friend and her magickal home, which was filled with creative wonder. I brought with me a meditation I had written, which felt appropriate for grounding and connecting for the work ahead. It was a guided visualization to journey to the edge of the underworld to meet with loved ones lost. We went home with bits of plaid cloth to unravel, for the art of fringed edges. These tiny details would be woven into a stunning tribute.

The next day, after coffee and a bit of unraveling, we were delighted to be delivered and guided through a local treasure, Lowe Mill ARTS & Entertainment. To our surprise, we had wandered into an impromptu art-cation! Our mystical guide led us through rows of interesting and wonderful art galleries throughout three floors of market space. We got to meet several artists and had a bit of a shopping frenzy with one artist who *wowed* us with the beauty of her work. We also got a sneak peek at a bit of art in chocolate that would be a sweet focal point of the celebration. Handcrafted chocolate truffles sealed with a kiss from our sacred celebrant. His signature was pressed into a crowning coin of chocolate (like sealing wax on an important royal document), then dusted with gold. Seriously, this man must have lived well to have been so loved.

That night, we gathered with more family and friends in the home that had been prepared for his comfort. He died just days before the planned move. They had hoped to "come home" to a space outfitted for the many needs of a paraplegic. We met people whose names we had seen attached to loving comments. Together we watched social media with dedication for the hopeful delivery of miraculous news. We sometimes witnessed triumphs and finally . . . heartbreak. We did not know their faces, but we knew the depth of their devotion. These were the ones who never left, even when things got hard. They served in every way possible, a man whose body was broken. And supported his wife whose courageous heart moved through backbreaking days and sleepless nights to ensure his safety and survival. These people whom we were blessed to meet, exceed the definition of friendship. They held space through a seven-year saga of trial and tribulation. They witnessed their friends losing a home to the burden of medical bills, packing, and moving more than once—not to mention all that goes into supporting the needs of someone whose body no longer can do what was once expected. This loving community encircled this sacred family and did whatever was needed to allow them to focus on the important work required.

Then, the big day arrived. Together, we went with new friends and (re)claimed family to meet and dress the sacred space of celebration. My favorite tomboy and I loved getting to be a part of nurturing the vision dreamed up with great detail by this group of goddesses. Onto each round table went a black cloth that draped to the floor, a grey square of felt topped by hand-fringed flannel in green, black, and gray plaid. On top of that, an earthen vase of moss covered sticks encircled by seven white candles and a ring of green and white sea glass. As we worked on the tables, another friend arranged homegrown pale green hydrangeas for the altar, and smaller clusters were added to the stick vases.

There were so many delightful details involved in this mindful manifestation. There was a sweet slideshow of a life well lived projected onto a freshly painted wall. To the left was the altar. It held rich fabrics adorned with a huge arrangement of hydrangeas, his glasses and watch encased in a dome of glass, a white candle— a beacon to call his spirit home, and a shot of Irish whiskey as a sacred offering. The altar sat beneath a portrait of Himself, painted by a friend after his passing. It depicted a scene captured in a photograph during their journey to Ireland, when he stood regally upon the Hill of Tara, where the High Kings were once crowned.

We lunched and rested, then returned to the venue to greet the guests. A trio of musicians enchanted the hall with Celtic music and Irish folk songs throughout the evening. And once those who had gathered in memorium had settled in with snacks and beverages, we learned more about the man we honored. The evening's emcee was a friend who had searched, purchased, and literally furnished the home of her friend, so she could focus on caregiving. The Huntsville Feminist Choir performed two songs dedicated to the memory of one of their biggest supporters. Friends and family members stood up to speak about a man they respected, admired, loved, and deeply missed. Energy was raised in laughter, as we learned of pranks and puns. Everyone in the room was brought to tears by the words of gratitude expressed by one of his final caregivers. She told us of how she insisted on giving his family a much-needed break—despite his protests. As she bathed and nurtured his body, he fortified her esteem and encouraged her efforts to further her education. As she lifted her eyes to the heavens and announced to him the educational grant she just won with gratitude for his support, our eyes released the emotion we'd all been holding.

This last tribute reminded me of my dad's stay in rehab last year. He told me about one of his attendants, who recently immigrated for a better life. She had been worried about an English test she would have to pass to move forward with her education to become a nurse, and Dad had offered words of encouragement and to help her practice. The day he told me the story, with tears in his eyes, he announced that she came in to tell him she had passed the test. I know that we all hope to feel like we've made a difference in the lives of others, and I know that the man we honored that night would have been enormously proud of his caregiver. He would have understood the multitude of ways that he made a difference in the lives of many.

Though we never knew him, my favorite tomboy and I got to know him through stories shared. Most of all, we understood his strength of character, his warmth of compassion, his generosity of kindness, and his wicked and wonderful sense of humor. We got to know the purity of his integrity through witnessing such grace in those whom he loved.

At the end of the evening, we gathered into a circle and raised a parting glass filled with a shot of Jameson's Irish Whiskey. The Celtic Trio played that well-known tune as we held up our offerings of remembrance and respect. We held sacred space for his devoted wife, still weary but growing stronger, his three heartbroken and adoring sons, two by birth and one by choice. We held space for his grandchildren and family present and those who wished to be there, but could not. And we held space for this remarkably loving and supportive community who held this family in their safe keeping through many difficult days and years. Until, finally peace was found at the High King's crossing into the Summerland.

Here's to cheating, stealing and drinking. For if you cheat, may you cheat death. And if you steal, may

you steal a maiden's heart. And if you drink, may
you drink with me! - Irish Blessing

We shared another day of restful togetherness before my
lifelong friend and I got back on the plane to come home. It was a
surreal parting, for we had come to feel as if we belonged there
among these remarkable and loving souls. How special, for a
woman in her grief to make us feel so welcome and at home. Of the
lifetime of memories that my favorite tomboy and I share, I am
certain that this holy weekend when we were witness to true grace,
will remain one of our favorites.

Somewhere in the conversation of these four days, I reminded
my favorite tomboy that I intend to go first, for I cannot fathom
living a single day without her. How lucky am I to have been given
the profound gift of her friendship, and that she should share so
generously with me the honor of knowing and loving her family,
too.

At 1 a.m., I walked into my parents' home, having come
straight from the airport. I emptied my father's catheter bag and
helped him into his pajamas, gave him his evening pills, stood with
the spit cup and the rinse cup while he brushed his teeth. I then
made sure the doors were closed and locked before making my way
up the street to my house and my waiting cat. As I climbed into
bed, I reflected on the years of service our cousin/friend had
devoted to the man we had just honored. I smiled with gratitude
for the blessing of being able to do the same for my parents and for
the love and devotion of our own community who are presently
holding space for us. We are so blessed.

Thank you for walking this path with me. I'm so happy you
are here. If I could, I would share one of those intoxicating truffles
with you. Cheers!

Holding On and Letting Go – September 2019

My average day begins too early to rise, so I look through my memories on Facebook for inspiration. I then either share the original post or create a piece of art to share by placing a quote that resonated with me years ago onto a photograph that resonates today. By now, my ragamuffin kitty, Morgan, has decided it is time for me to get out of bed and serve her breakfast and offer her my chest to purr upon.

I put the water on to boil and place her dish of hope onto the spot reserved for her meals. I hope she will eat what I have selected for her today. I then make my pour over coffee and sit down for morning reading. By the time I have finished my coffee, it is time to head over to serve my stud muffin. Just kidding, it's my dad.

I usually arrive to find him working a puzzle on his tablet, while listening to music or a tv show playing in the foreground. He smiles when he finally looks up to greet me. This is the picture I will carry with me for all of my days. I hand him his water mug and feed him his morning meds.

Next is the breakfast inquiry. Will it be a bagel with cream cheese? Will it be Italian toast with butter and jam (not jelly! jam)? I put the bagel in the toaster and start the coffee. At this time, evidence of other life in the house emerges. Two small dogs, one midsize dog, followed by Mom in her nightgown. We all say good morning, and get on with our daily ritual.

Dad gets his bagel and an Ensure for extra protein. When coffee is half brewed, Mom and Dad are each served a cup. I do a little tidying on the kitchen chaos (my least favorite task, next to filing), and once everyone is settled in, I head out the door receiving gratitude and a "drive careful" from Dad. This blessing comes whether I am driving or walking exactly seven houses east of theirs.

Today, I will go back at noon to help Dad with a bath. We had one of the three bathrooms in the house outfitted for his care. It has a walk-in tub, a taller toilet with bidet, and now it has what I call a toilet corral. There are bars everywhere, to assist Dad with safe movement through the space where his walker will not go. Strategically installed, he is able to push himself (with a bit of struggle) to standing, and pull himself forward. Since he also has a loss of dexterity in his hands, we are able to assist with hygiene and wound care (pressure sores from sitting and thinning skin) from this station.

When he carefully steps into his tub, we will close the door and fill it with warm water. As it fills, I can use the sprayer to wet and wash his hair. Then, when the water is above the jet ports, he can relax for a bit as the warm water massages his aching and fatigued body. Last week, we received help with this task, when I asked if we could add more assistance to his home care. He has physical therapy twice a week, and a wound care nurse comes once a week. What I found, as I was going over our routine with the aid was that I didn't want to give this up!

I know that I will not always be able to do this all by myself, but when it comes down to asking for help and receiving it . . . I am quite certain that no one can care for my father as well as I. The thing is, helping him out of the tub has become more difficult. Standing up to exit the tub is more challenging than before, and I cannot always get him to his feet alone. My father is six feet tall and somewhere under 200 pounds. But still . . . that bath time is divine, and I am not willing to allow him to forego it—even if I can only get him in there once a week (like a defiant toddler).

Next comes getting him dressed. Last week, the aid had to dash off to help another, and so we finished the bath time ritual on our own. Getting him slowly to his lift chair, then pulling flannel pajamas over his feet and up to his knees. Followed by the excruciating struggle to stand again after so much work getting in and out of the tub—and finally pulling up the pajamas so he can finally sit down for a long rest. Seated, we can do the rest. Shirt over the head and reaching through the arm holes to find his clenched fists. Using a trick a nurse taught me in pre-op to get his compression socks on by placing a plastic baggie over his toes, then pulling it off through the hole. And finally, putting on socks with nonskid soles—to keep him just a little safer between recliner and bathroom travels.

Today, Kelly and Jodie will come for PT and wound care. We love how they love him. I will stop by to see if I can get him to eat, or at least to consume another Ensure. He's not very good with the fluid consumption when getting up to pee is like a hero's journey, so I've been tricking him with a big bowl of watermelon in the late afternoon. Then I go back in the evening to "tuck them in." I fix Dad something to eat, if he'll have it, and give him his evening pills. If he's up to it, we'll do another trip to the bathroom before I lock up and go home to bed.

A couple of days ago, while waiting for Hurricane Dorian to arrive (gratefully, he took a detour and stayed to the East of us), my phone rang at 3:30 a.m. I picked up the call and said, "Hold on, Dad. I'm coming!"

I know it is Dad when the display reads: Mom's Cell. I had my brother surround the house in Alexa dots, and he programmed them to dial my number if Dad asked her to call me. I have one next to his chair and now I have one in the bathroom, too. When I arrived, two minutes later—groggy, but sure to grab my keys this time, instead of my pendulum as I dashed out the door—he was on the floor in the living room.

Mom is hearing impaired, and could not hear him call. Without panic, I went to the IndeeLift we keep plugged in nearby, and I rolled it over to him so he could hand walk himself back onto the platform. Then, he slowly rose from the ground as I pressed the arrow *up*. With the use of his walker, we finished what he started; an early morning trip to the potty. Mom woke up and, by the time we had Dad settled back into his recliner, we were all pretty much awake but grateful that this was a pretty low drama moment. No blood. No mess. Just a whole lot of body betrayal to battle and overcome.

Dad apologizes when he has to call, and I remind him that this is exactly why I have chosen not to go back to work. It is his job to call me when he is in need, and it is my job to respond to the best of my ability. This is by far, the most important and rewarding work I've done. I can remember the sense of urgency and the heaviness I felt while supporting the head of HR who was responsible for the CEO succession plan for a Fortune 500 company. There were many days that I cried from the stress of it all. Did I leave anything on the copy machine that may give away the idea that a sixty-five-year-old man in waning health might actually retire someday? It could cause the corporate stock to plummet! How silly that seems to me now. Who cares, really? I will never understand how corporations have become more important than people.

I have shed my concern for the shareholder and given everything now to my most beloved care holders—the people who raised me. Both social workers for their entire careers, they taught me the importance of community care and respecting the dignity of all beings. They deserve to receive the care they offered to others, and I'll be sure they get it.

Now, you'll have to excuse me. It's bath time! "Hold on, Dad. I'm coming!"

The Love of a Good Cat – September 2019

Every joint in my body aches this morning. I cannot get them to relax. That would require informing my body that she is gone, and that there is nothing left to hold onto. Perhaps it is my empathy out of balance, and rigor has set in like the rigid nature of her sacred vessel that I carried in for aftercare as soon as the doors opened five hours after she left me. Like three times before, "Can you please help my baby get to Greenbriar (the pet crematorium)?"

Yesterday was an excruciatingly long day. I left her for only moments to tend to my father a few doors down. Otherwise, there were only a couple of times that I let her escape my embrace.

She had stopped eating, and the medication the doctor gave us didn't help. My home looks like triage, with failed attempts to save a life scattered everywhere. IV fluids hang on a hook next to the couch, a syringe with water to stave off thirst on the ottoman, six different plates and bowls on the floor offer unconsumed food remnants that begged for an appetite. "Okay, how about filet mignon? No? Then, let's try scrambled egg with your favorite cheese. No? Well, how about . . . "

I spoke to her doctor that morning and learned that, though she had delivered peace to two of my darlings in years past, she could no longer bear to be the bringer of death. She referred me to another, who happened to be out of the country. So . . . the Universe had spoken. We would be doing this the old-fashioned way. With patience, with reverence, and with so much love.

So, I gave Dad his morning meds and served him breakfast and informed my parents I would not be back unless they needed me. I walked in the door and Morgan, my kitty, did not run to greet me. So, I ran to greet her, instead. I picked her up and returned her to my chest, where we would remain until the end.

When I wrote about my experiences with death last year, as a part of a death doula curriculum, I introduced my readers to Morgan. She came to me six years ago with her brother, Arthur. He died tragically four years ago and since then, Morgan and I have lived a peaceful and mindful existence.

She blossomed when he left us, for he had been the alpha cat (I guess). He was a bit of a bully, really, and I hated that she was submissive to him. She and I fell madly in love in those days that followed, and I'm not sure I have ever known a more kind and gentle soul than she. She would greet me at the door upon entering, and when I picked her up, she would place her paws on each side of my neck and rub her cheek against my nose. She would mark me for all to know that I belonged to her. I was her human.

She would wake me in the mornings by climbing over me and settling next to my face for my cat tongue facials, which I referred to as Morganderm Abrasion. I would turn my face to be sure she didn't miss a spot. If I didn't rise by the time she was through, she would walk over me to stand behind me and poke me with her paw until I gave in. She didn't always have an empty plate, either.

Morgan had grown thin over the last year following a stroke-like event that left her with a slight head tremor. This is when she seemed to forget how to drink properly from the fountain, and she would dunk her head beneath the running water. I would see her with ruffled brow, and slick back the water in her fur to help her with a little impromptu bath. There was a change in the sound of the falling water whenever she did this odd bow, and I heard that noise prolonged the day before I knew she was leaving. It was my portend of what was to come.

As she lay in my arms, nearing her final breaths, I scrolled through photos of when I first brought her home with Arthur. I couldn't believe how full she was. I nicknamed her my Squishy. In the mornings, as she stood at the corner of my bed, I would lean over and envelope her with my arms and bury my face in her fur, kissing her cheek a hundred times. I could hear her protest, as if to say, "Oh, mother. Too much love. Give me more."

She was seventeen pounds after a year in my care, and this year . . . she was down to seven. I could feel her shoulder bones the way that I feel my father's shoulder bones, and I can see how we are at times larger than life, and as we near the end our bodies let go of old baggage. Perhaps it makes us easier to care for, the lighter we become. It was an odd thing to stop worrying about feeding each too much, to start wanting them to eat more of anything that might add weight.

It is a mean thing that nature does to us, to bring into our lives such sacred beings who don't get to stay very long. Six years was not enough, Morgan, for my aching heart. I need a hundred more!

She was my comforter through so much loss (Arthur, the boss who loved me, my former identity). And now my only comfort is knowing that I served her well. I loved her completely. I held her tiny, sacred being in my arms for nearly twenty hours. I was her doula as she transitioned from my world into the light of all that is. I instructed her on where to go and who to look for, and I asked forgiveness for the things I failed to do because I did not understand her language and couldn't see what was going on inside that precious water-soaked head.

Morgan came into my life when her elderly owner could no longer care for her. It was three months after Nightshade died. My only regret, is that I was not ready sooner, for I could have had more Morgan and Arthur, and my life would have been even richer.

I know that I will rescue again and, without a doubt, I will be rescued in return. But first, I will take time to sit in solitude with my sweet angel kitty. When she shows up, I don't want to mistake her energy for that of another. She was given wings at birth, you know. Morgan was a Turkish Van cat. Their distinct markings are a mostly white body with ears and tail of orange or black, with a spot between the shoulders that is called the mark of Allah. Morgan's mark was a pair of orange angel wings. She lived with purpose and fulfilled her mission. And she has taken flight . . . returning to the light of truth.

Oh, how blessed we are to be chosen by these furry beings of love and light. They were given the power to dispel darkness, and they so freely share their magick with us. This truth is what encourages us to break our own hearts over and over again. We would dwell in the dark without their light. With that kind of love, everything is illuminated.

This ache is all consuming. I wonder how long it will stay with me. My muscles and joints feel as if they are still holding on. I guess I must get to the work of letting go. As I said to her, "It's okay to let go. You are safe. Mom's not going anywhere, and she will miss you every day of her life, but she will be okay, too." Into the light of truth, we go.

Eldercare Blessings – October 2019

If we can recognize grace in the arrival of a new person in our lives, who delivers the care and wisdom that we did not even know we needed, we must also recognize the arrival of tools and devices that have been discovered to improve the quality of our lives.

The last year has been particularly challenging due to a series of events, some of which I'm not completely clear. Pop had some heart tests done a couple of years ago, which resulted in prescriptions for medication to lower his blood pressure and cholesterol. Things seemed fine for a while, until he started falling down. Long story short, his blood pressure was so low that he would black out and fall to the floor.

One of those falls last year led to scar tissue in his urethra, which was finally repaired this summer. The consequences of these falls, the muscle weakness, the difficulty in mobility, are that Pop simply chooses to move less. Less movement, less effort, less risk.

Of course, this causes other issues, and the biggest one for Pop has been pressure sores. The first wound that came to light was while in rehab after the fall that delivered the stricture. Looking at the calendar, I can conclude that this started in October of 2018, and a year later, we have finally found relief.

This tale is not to go into the gory details and drawn out story of all of our struggles, but to share with others the glorious tools that have come into our lives to ease our burdens and literally, heal our wounds.

So, here's a list of items that we cannot live without.
1. The Rollator
2. The Transport Chair
3. The Lift Recliner
4. Bathroom Safety Grab Bars
5. The Walk-In Tub
6. IndeeLift
7. Pneumatic Air Pad Medical Cushion
8. Medihoney Gel

Each time we have found a resource, device, or product that has delivered comfort and improvement for Pop's wellness and a bit of ease to the concerns of his caregivers (my mother and me), we have done a little happy dance.

Dad's had a progression of walkers over the years and we love the one he has now, which provides decent stability for a guy who is six feet tall and can't feel his feet or legs. The Nitro Rollator is our favorite, so far.

Having a lightweight transport chair has made going to doctor appointments so much easier. The fear of him falling should his knee or ankle drop out is alleviated for us both. It has gotten hard for him to get out of it because he is tall and the seat is low, but we've remedied that problem with a four-inch seat cushion, and lessons from his physical therapist who comes to the house twice every week. The one we have is only twelve pounds, and even mom can fold it and lift it into her Prius Hatchback.

The lift recliner was an item we held off on, because Pop wanted to use his own strength for as long as he was able. But now he uses it to rise, and I have to remind him that it is as high as it will go, and he can stop pushing the *up* button. Ha! We originally ordered one from a well-known recliner/furniture store, but once it was home, we didn't love it. It didn't elevate his feet enough. So, Mom ordered another one from a catalog, and it works much better.

The Bathroom Safety Grab Bars are a *must*! As our muscles lose strength, the act of rising from a seated position can be challenging. Our dear friend shared his secret weapon with us. A local superhero who installs safety features. We live in Central Florida, and were delighted when Ron from Install Don't Fall came to the house, walked into the bathroom with Pop, and asked all of the right questions. When I visited later that day, the bathroom was outfitted with everything my father needed for safe and secure passage throughout the bathroom, where his walker will not easily fit.

The Walk-In Tub is a wonderful thing! It is still not easy for Pop to enter and exit, due to his mobility issues, but with gentle steps and grab bars in all the right places, he can step in, close the door, and let warm water rise to soothe his aching joints. I help him wash his hair, and he can handle the rest with the help of the jets that improve circulation in his legs, a sponge, and the liquid soap dispenser that is within his reach. We were not entirely thrilled with the installation, so I'm not going to advertise the company, but we will definitely sing the praises of this investment, which included an upgraded toilet with bidet and cleansing feature.

After our third or fourth call to 911 for a "Lift Assist" when Pop had fallen to the floor and Mom and I could not help him up, I found the IndeeLift through an online search. This tool is amazing. It is as compact as a dolly/hand truck, and can be unplugged and rolled to wherever Pop has fallen (even in the bathroom), and as long as he can scoot back onto the platform, we can press a button to bring his knees to a ninety-degree angle, and help him rise to his walker and back into his recliner. I *love* this tool!

The most recent acquisition for our eldercare tool belt has been the Pneumatic Air Pad Medical Cushion by MobiCushion. Mom found it on a search when I was feeling overwhelmed by these wounds that seemed they would never heal. Since Pop has chosen to stay in his recliner rather than sleeping in his bed, I was prepared to turn his office into a hospital room, with a bed that would allow him to roll onto his side once in a while. I knew of the air mattresses that alternate pressure that Dad has had prescribed in the hospital. But he was unwilling to give up sleeping in his recliner. Within minutes, Mom had ordered this item and I set it up upon delivery. Let me tell you . . . the wounds that had been varying degrees of "almost healed" to "horrifyingly deep" over the last year, were *completely healed* within a week. Not exaggerating . . . one week.

One last item that we've learned about in the last year is also for wound care, and it made a miraculous difference in healing time for Pop's pressure wounds. I'd imagine it works the same for any injury of an open and bloody nature. Medihoney goes right onto a wound and delivers immediate relief and rapid healing. Although Pop's wounds kept coming back over the last year (before the magic cushion), they would be well-nurtured by this healing salve. And of course, we always knew that honeybees were magickal (wink: Melissa means honeybee in Greek).

Oh! I almost forgot. I am not a fan of the Alexa AI system (having a strong sense of logic and having seen the movie *2001: A Space Odyssey* at a young age), but my brother did install a few dots around my parents' home and Dad will have Alexa call me if he has fallen and needs assistance. For us, it is easier than paying for a system with a middleman, so to speak. I can be there in less than two minutes when he calls.

I'm heading over to check on Pop now, but it is my hope that something in this post will deliver hope and peace to another caregiver who is struggling with keeping a loved one safe and well. And to those caregivers, I offer my blessings, my reverence, and my gratitude for the love you offer which makes this difficult journey less fearful for each sacred soul you serve.

Waves of Sorrow and Bliss – October 2019

I have been feeling a little lost, as of late. Oh, I'm doing my usual routine . . . wake early and marry a quote to a photo for some kind of inspirational and positive message to share with others, get out of bed, make coffee and check in on the world through social media, then check on Pop to give him his pills and feed him breakfast. But then, I come home and . . . that's kind of it. I feel as if I should be doing more with my time. I have managed to write a blog post or work on a mission statement to guide and support others (a part of the homework for a workshop I'm facilitating), and I've written a meditation for my upcoming *Samhain* retreat, but I am also sleeping . . . a lot.

More than one friend reminds me that I am grieving. Odd that one would have to be reminded. The day after tomorrow will be exactly one month from when I placed Morgan on my chest and held her for twenty hours straight until she took her last breath, and I finally let her tiny sacred vessel leave my embrace.

I don't necessarily feel that I'm thinking about it all the time, but I am certainly feeling her absence. I still open the door carefully to see if she is there to greet me and to be sure she doesn't get frisky and try to dash outside. And every time I enter the kitchen, I look down to be sure she hasn't magickally appeared behind me, so not to step on her.

If you have been here before, you might notice the quiet where her drinking fountain once trickled, but you might also still expect to see her in her favorite spot—at the window seat in the library. You see, I have not been able to bring myself to vacuum. The blanket and brush she and I curled up with on that final day, remains right where we left them. The tiny stool she would perch upon for tiny cat naps is covered in fluff. I know that normal people would have done this particular housework weeks ago, but I am not ready.

Today, my friend asked me to run by his house to pick up a package that was delivered. Morgan and I had stayed there for a few days at the end of August. I had been terribly stressed about taking her out of the house while work was being done—her safe place, but she surprised me. I let her out of her crate, in which she did *not* wet herself from anxiety of travel (for the first time ever), and she explored my friends' home with curiosity and without fear. I would come back from checking on my parents and enter the home to find her napping on the third step up the stairs. It felt as if we were taking our first vacation together. It's a nice memory to have between us.

As I drove to my friends' house, I thought about our little vacation, and that spot upon the stairs, and the tiny tufts of white fluff that I meant to return to vacuum up, but then . . . she died . . . and time stopped and sped up, all at once. I think I lost days in my consciousness. I considered going inside to see if I could find any signs of Morgan within, but decided against it. My next visit will have to be when my friends are back with their three pugs, because two houses without Morgan is just too much emptiness to bear.

Another friend lost her beloved mother this week. It was such a rapid decline; I can imagine she must feel a strange combination of shock and relief. The diagnosis, which explained a drastic and worrisome change in her behavior this summer, was a brain tumor that had previously worn a costume of Alzheimer's Disease. Once the curtain was dropped and the truth was revealed, her mother was placed in the angelic care of hospice and transitioned peacefully within a week. A blessing, I believe, when the brain and body are no longer communicating effectively. My friend has been very ill for the past two weeks, and I hope that she is finding comfort in healing, and peace in the knowledge that the one she loves no longer struggles with that conflict.

When her mother went to hospice, I adapted the *phowa* practice from the *Tibetan Book of Living and Dying* for her and her husband to recite throughout transition. I invited them to say the words that I had also offered for the nephew of my favorite tomboy last summer.

It is such an odd thing, the way that a being goes from being physically in your life every day, to being completely absent in an instant. We are left to fill the void they've left behind, yet our minds cannot fathom bridging that chasm. I think that's what this feeling must be . . . this strange space of going through the motions without getting much done. We are in this cat shaped hole, or mother shaped hole, without a clue as to how to fill it so that we can climb back to the surface.

Here's the thing, though. I love the darkness. As we move into the dark part of the year with waning daylight, I welcome the cloak of Mother Darkness to wrap me in quiet, in peace, in introspection, in healing, in comfort, even in aloneness (which is very different from loneliness). To me, this is where transformation resides. When we who grieve are ready, we will fill the holes our loved ones have left behind with the light of joyful memory. When the time is right, we will emerge from the darkness renewed. The sorrow and the bliss will weave together, a cloak of transformation made by love.

So, if you come by for a visit any time soon, expect to see some white fluff about. For now, it reminds me of her terrible absence, but it also reminds me that she was once here. And I won't stop listening for her tiny voice. I was certain I heard it this morning as I stepped into the shower.

Finally, we have signs in our neighborhood that warn about urban coyotes. In fact, my two neighbors with cats—who have been outdoor cats (by choice) for more than a decade—reported they were both lost within weeks of each other. Every time I see that sign, I think of how lucky I was to hold Morgan right through to the end.

It rained all night last night, and when I walked out to my car this morning, I saw paw prints on the sidewalk. They were larger than the usual suspect (I have seen cats, opossum, and raccoons in the area), and I gathered this was the closest I would get to a coyote sighting. So, of course . . . I looked it up. And here's what it says:

> The coyote spirit animal makes itself known when you feel like you have lost your way. The coyote symbolism signifies the answers to your problems that often come in ways and forms you least expect.

Perhaps I have lost my way, for a little while. But this is temporary. I am sitting with the silence and honoring this moment. If I look for her in my mind's eye, she is everywhere all at once. She is in the library window seat and she is in the kitchen. She is marching up the steps to my bed and she is right next to me on the couch. There is evidence of her on every surface, so I know that she was just here. When she's ready, she will climb back onto my chest to purr, and I will wrap her in my cloak of love and perhaps we'll take a nap.

Centering Our Souls at *Samhain* – November 2019

Of the workshops I created in 2019, this was a part of the Retreat Weekend I manifested with the help of a few friends. The theme was ultimately to connect with our lost loved ones, while the veil between the worlds was thin.

At the heart of this retreat was the myth of Persephone; you know the story of my dedication to her while studying end-of-life care. To set up our time with the goddess of the underworld for my guests, I shared my preferred version of the tale with a bit more flair in order to make them feel safe on our shared journey.

> Persephone was in a field collecting flowers to make a circlet for her mother's hair, when she came upon a lost soul who could not find the doorway to the underworld. She returned to her mother, the Goddess Demeter, and told her that she must go into the underworld to guide these lost souls and offer them initiation. Though She did not want to let her go (the plight of most mothers), Demeter watched Persephone's descent and immediately longed for her return. As she mourned the absence of her daughter, the world fell into a stark, quiet version of itself as a blanket of snow fell and the flowers receded into the earth.
>
> Meanwhile, Persephone took Her place at the crystal doorway to offer seeds of transformation to those who no longer walked upon the earth. Initiation involved consumption of a pomegranate seed, and these garnet seeds would light the inner flame of those moving into a new way of being. When Persephone returned from the underworld to visit her mother, Demeter felt such joy that the earth burst forth in blossoms of celebration, as life and color bloomed once more.

Here, we have a story of creation and of changing seasons, mothers and daughters, of love and loss, of passion and responsibility, of transformation, death and renewal. This is a version of an ancient tale to which I can relate.

My current belief (current—because I am ever evolving based on my own life experience) about the transformation that death brings is that we are all energetic beings. In this human incarnation we are able to learn and grow through emotions that are not experienced beyond the confines of the body. So, once we have gathered these lessons and intentions, we are free to leave the body behind as we return to energetic form. Those we love and have lost in body to death, remain ever present in energetic form. My intention for connecting with our lost loves at *Samhain*, was to use the tool of creative visualization or meditation to sit with them once more.

And so, it was Persephone who manifested within the cave of sacred memory to offer us initiation and safe passage. When we reached the central chamber, which was warmed by firelight with walls donned with portraits of our ancestors and dear ones lost, we sat upon a crimson couch and welcomed whomever chose to step through the doorway veiled in magickal moonlight.

The results of meditation differ, based on experience. Someone who is well practiced may have honed the ability to get out of their own way to let vision come and let judgment or expectation fall away. But one should never negate the vision or experience they find in the sacred space of the powerful mind.

JK Rowling, I feel, captured it perfectly in *The Deathly Hallows*, when Harry asks the ghostly image of Professor Dumbledore:

> "Tell me one last thing," said Harry. "Is this real? Or has this been happening inside my head?"
>
> "Of course, it is happening inside your head, Harry, but why on earth should that mean that it is not real?"

Some of us had very clear, even life altering conversations with one or more people on that comfy couch. Some of us saw ourselves surrounded by smiling loved ones who were present, without words. As for me, I found an opportunity to seek forgiveness and receive acceptance at the edge of the underworld.

I had no expectation of my own personal journey, since I had written the meditation, led the visualization, and was ultimately holding space for the experience of others. However, as I provided the silent pause for those on this journey to find connection, Kirby came through the veil for me.

He was smiling and happy to see me, and the feeling was mutual. A part of my guidance was to consider the conversations we never got to have . . . the ones where we have the opportunity to say to our loved ones: please forgive me. I forgive you. Thank you. I love you. Twenty-six years have passed since Kirby left this earthly realm, and he came through so that I could tell him something I needed to say.

When I was twenty-four, I had not yet learned about life, let alone death. I had minimal access to my gift for words. When I sat with him, whether in his home or in the hospital, I felt a complete lack. I did not know what to say or how to say it. I sat and held his hand and looked into his eyes, but I always felt that I provided little comfort. But here's the thing I've carried . . . shame. When I held his hand as he lay in his hospital bed, lung capacity too weak to push out words, I was not fully present. As I held his hand, I thought about the fear I carried for a disease on which I had been well educated. I knew that holding his hand was zero risk for my wellness, yet I can recall leaving the room and washing my hands with urgency. The only real threat was to him . . . my germs could compromise his health and not the other way around. I would give anything to be able to sit with him again with the presence, compassion, and understanding I now possess.

I asked Kirby for his forgiveness and, even now, I can almost hear his voice, "Oh, Melissa. There is nothing to forgive!" As he tilts his head, glances at me with compassion, and offers me that gorgeous grin . . . tears flow, and I know that this is happening inside my head, and also, that this is real.

When I lead a meditation, my main worry is whether the silence I offer is long enough for a message to be received, or so long that I lose the mindful attention of those I'm hoping to lead. When Kirby faded into the veil, I ended the silence with these words . . .

We know that time moves differently in the Underworld, and though we long to be with our loved ones, we know that now is not that time. Tonight is a moment when time stands still, and here we were blessed to connect between the worlds. But time will move on and we shall go with it. Much like when we connect in the realm of the living, it feels as if no time has passed . . . so will be the day when they come to greet us and take us from the temporary realm to the eternal. Until then, we honor them by choosing to live in joy and happiness. It would be an insult to their sacrifice not to.

We made our way out of sacred space the same way we came in, and we shared the stories of our experience. We cried together, and we amazed one another with knowledge of healing offered and received between the worlds.

The next day, a meditation informed everyone of a gift from Persephone. We were all given a garnet pomegranate seed in the form of a teardrop bead attached to a small silver ring. The symbolism was that we would be offered safe passage any time we wished to connect with our loved ones, and when our time comes, we, too, will be received and initiated by Her love.

We then took the gift we were given and selected a series of other beads to encircle our wrists in the form of a bracelet that would forever remind us of this time we've shared at the edge of the underworld.

The final piece of the remembrance portion of the retreat was to write the names of those we had invoked onto gathered autumn leaves. We drove to a nearby river, walked to the center of the bridge, and blew kisses into the wind as our leaves floated down and around, returning our beloveds to the eternal flow of the river that separates us.

When we returned to the mountain house we now recognized as home, some of us stepped into the kitchen and continued the preparation of a true Thanks-Giving meal. When my hosts suggested a full turkey dinner with all the sides, I thought it sounded great, but I hadn't really considered the symbolism.

We were at the end of our time together. We twelve had chosen to be vulnerable and authentic. We supported and celebrated transition and transformation. We had a conversation with Death and found ourselves more determined to live. We cried together, and we built a bond that transcends time and space. We agreed that we wanted to do this again. And we gave thanks for all of it.

The day before these gorgeous beings gathered, I started a seven-month course on Holding Space Leadership, and our course creator and guide, Heather Plett, shared with us a poem. As she read these words, I understood that I would share them, too. They are perfection. So, before we sat down to our final full-togetherness, I read these words to my courageous and wonderful guests, and now . . . I offer them to you.

"Blessing for a New Beginning" by John O'Donohue

In out of the way places of the heart
Where your thoughts never think to wander
This beginning has been quietly forming
Waiting until you were ready to emerge.

For a long time it has watched your desire
Feeling the emptiness grow inside you
Noticing how you willed yourself on
Still unable to leave what you had outgrown.

It watched you play with the seduction of safety
And the grey promises that sameness whispered
Heard the waves of turmoil rise and relent
Wondered would you always live like this.

Then the delight, when your courage kindled,
And out you stepped onto new ground,
Your eyes young again with energy and dream
A path of plenitude opening before you.

Though your destination is not yet clear
You can trust the promise of this opening;
Unfurl yourself into the grace of beginning
That is at one with your life's desire.

Awaken your spirit to adventure
Hold nothing back, learn to find ease in risk
Soon you will be home in a new rhythm
For your soul senses the world that awaits you.

Each farewell the next morning took away a little piece of my heart in the form of longing and protection. And by noon, we were three again. We set to the task of breaking the set and packing it up. Our journey down the mountain would come the next morning, and there was much to do.

Gratefully, the Universe rewarded me with a little more time with my dear hosts, who drove over from their daughter's home. I was pleased to share my gratitude for the remarkable journey we had all shared in this beautiful space that held us all in warmth and love. And because it is what sacred gardeners do, I planted seeds of intention for two retreats in 2020. My lifelong friend took notes during our eleven-hour drive home, on our ideas for how to manifest more self-love at *Beltane* next May. I can't wait to light that candle and dedicate that hearth to bless, once again, the journey we will share.

Of course, there were no retreats in 2020. We met to set our intentions at *Imbolc* in February, and then the world shut down in response to COVID-19. I didn't do a lot of writing that year. My world grew very small in order to keep my parents safe. I considered it a great blessing that both of my parents had remained relatively well, with no need to become one of many who would go to the hospital or rehab alone because of safety restrictions. Until October.

Time for Mending – October 2020

One week ago today, my phone rang at 7:37 a.m. Three out of the four other times that week that my phone rang was in the hour of two in the morning, so I'm pretty sure my body thought it was home free, for the night, from the trauma of what those calls announced.

When the caller ID says it is "Mom's Cell" calling, I know that Alexa is calling me from my father's bathroom. It informs me that my larger-than-life, eighty-three-year-old father is lying on the floor and that he needs my assistance.

This fifth call in a week wasn't really a surprise. His Leo's pride kept him from calling me *before* he pushed the button of his lift chair to bring him to his feet (he didn't want to wake me), and then pull his red Rollator Nitro walker before him so he could struggle to rise and make his way to the bathroom to empty his bladder. Had he called, I could have been unlocking the front door of my parents' home before he released the brakes to step gingerly away from the safety of his recliner.

Instead, I got the familiar call that puts my body into a trauma response. Wondering where on the floor I will find him, and if this will be the time that I am unable to help.

The fourth call was one of those times, actually. I pulled out the Indeelift device that helps us lift his body to find his feet, but he didn't have the strength to pull himself onto the platform. I had to call for a "lift assist," and the fire department sent over four strong men to set him back into his chair.

But the fifth call . . . this was the one we were all dreading. This was the one where he didn't get to decline a trip to the emergency room. This was the one where the pain was too great. This was the one that led to x-rays. This was the one that came with a diagnosis that comes with horror stories. My father, the man with bones and toenails of steel, had broken his hip.

I think he and I both went to that dark place with this news. I asked him what he was thinking, and he said that he was considering everything this would mean. He didn't elaborate, possibly because I was in tears considering the same thing, feeling as if I had failed to keep him safe. I was thinking that for years I'd heard it said, when an elderly person breaks a hip, they are not long for this world. He was probably thinking he should have called me before the trip rather than after the fall.

It would be twenty-four hours before they could do the surgery to put a rod in his leg and repair the break in his upper femur. I was grateful that COVID-19 restrictions allowed one visitor to stay with him in the ER and during visiting hours, once admitted. They gave him a pain blocker and some pain meds to get him through the night. As he was drifting off to sleep, and I wished him sweet dreams, he said to me, "We're going to have to get you one of those handheld crossbows." I'm not sure where those pain meds were taking him, but I wish I could have seen the view from his perspective.

On Sunday, he was accepted and transferred to a Rehabilitation Hospital that has a pretty strict regimen for recovery. They provide each patient with three hours per day of physical and occupational therapy. The intention is to have each patient out within two weeks. To be honest, I don't know that any amount of therapy will help. He has a host of complications that may impair the possibility of getting stronger. He fell four times in a week, and that was before he broke his hip. That said, before surgery I asked him if he wanted a DNR order should anything go wrong, and his response was a resounding, "*No!*" So, here's to the strength of spirit for something more.

As for me, I have not had a day off of caregiving duty since this time last year. In addition to wanting to stay close for the possibility of a 2 a.m. phone call, COVID-19 has never gone into remission in the state in which we live. It hasn't felt wise to travel and risk exposure or worse, unknowingly delivering the risk to others. Two-thousand-and-twenty has been a difficult year for all of us, and I have the added joy of constant highway construction just a few yards from my house. It's like living in a war zone with the sound of dump trucks banging like cannon fire, constant motion of cranes and power shovels, and then there's the rattle and hum that shakes the whole house and bounces the art off the walls as dirt is shimmied and compressed into a highway foundation. Oh! And the pounding of pylons! That felt like an all-out assault on my entire body. Needless to say, I'm exhausted.

One of the things I must acknowledge is that I have two significant strengths at play when it comes to my choice to not go back to work and care for my parents full-time. One is *empathy* and the other is *responsibility*. When I am more distressed about our current situation than either of my parents seem to be, it is quite possible that my strengths are out of balance.

I feel obligated to stand at attention and be of service. It's what I've always done. I used to get paid for it. Somehow, in my need to feel needed and worthy of love, I trained myself to give away so much of myself there was nothing left for me. The year my boss was dealing with a hostile takeover, I told myself I couldn't take time off unless she did, because it would cause *her* more stress. My own stress level and five weeks of unused vacation were secondary. Not because she required it of me, but because I demanded it of myself.

I've noticed how my body and mind have been telling me that it is time for a break, the way it did during that difficult year at work, but I hate that it may be made possible by my father's extended stay elsewhere to recover from a broken and mending body.

I'm working on figuring out how to get away during a pandemic, and plans are starting to develop. Meanwhile, I am mindful of how beautiful it can be to find oneself in need. During these months of lockdown, I have gotten to know my neighbors. Many of us have been here for decades, but the coming and going of our lives kept us passing with a wave or completely out of sight. Now, we have exchanged phone numbers, and text each other to see if anyone needs something from the store. And when a neighbor was outside the morning the ambulance came, I received messages of concern and outreach from several neighbors wanting to know that we are safe and well, and how they might be of service to me and my folks.

Dear friends and beloved community are letting us know that they are holding us close and they are standing by, intending to assist in any way. One friend thanked me for allowing her to cook a pot of soup for us this week. I thanked her back, for reminding me how important it is to allow those who love us to be of service when they desperately wish there was something they could do.

So, thank you, dear ones . . . for taking the time to read about the heavy burdens I carry, for sending your healing energy and caring thoughts for my father's recovery and wellness, and for holding space for a woman who is still learning how to treat herself with the same kindness and compassion she so abundantly offers to others. Much like the highway that runs through my side yard, I am a never-ending work in progress. It seems tedious, but worth the effort.

Thank you for walking this path with me. None of us should have to do the hard things alone. I suspect that when we feel that we are isolated or abandoned, it is because we are too overwhelmed to notice that we are surrounded by a tribe that has been paving the way all along. Goodness, we are so blessed, and ever so grateful. We hope that you and yours are safe and well.

After note:

My father stayed in rehab for a month. When it was clear that he would come home without the ability to walk, I set to the task of clearing out his office at home, to turn it into a hospital type bedroom.

I shared with friends on Facebook that Dad frequently told stories about his grandfather's garden in Massachusetts, a happy memory from childhood. I asked for anyone interested to send photos or canvas prints of flowers they had taken. I hoped to surprise my father with his own secret garden. I received so many wonderful replies, and my father came home to a room surrounded with flowers, butterflies, and the symbolic love and support of our beloved community. I am eternally grateful for every loving gesture we received.

The Empty Calendar – January 2021

Today, I pulled down the 2020 calendar to be replaced.

It was a gift from my financial advisor, featuring paintings from *The Saturday Evening Post*. Once upon a time, I would have passed on such a gift, seeking something more me . . . with artwork from a Pre-Raphaelite or something whimsical, but since I owe my current lifestyle, in part, to the compassionate insight of my financial advisor, I liked the idea of holding him close. (Thanks Tony!)

What a strange thing . . . to flip through the pages of a bygone calendar year like the one we've just narrowly escaped. To be honest, the world I manage resides mostly on Google, but the big things would usually go on the wall calendar. Like a visit from my brother and his family, a trip that might take me out of town, or a workshop I designed to share with others.

In this case, January reminded me of a friend's knee surgery, Second Sunday Supper, Book Group, and my fifty-first birthday. February boasted my second annual Seeds of Intention Workshop (where we would assess the different areas of our lives to determine where we wanted to focus our intentions for the year ahead), filing my taxes, and what would be the last time we would get to see my brother and his wife, who had come up from South Florida.

Then, I flip to March. It's kind of eerie to look at. There's a trip to San Antonio for a wedding, followed by a countdown. Fourteen days to wear a mask each time I entered my parents' home. Somewhere in my WordPress account, is an unfinished post about the beautiful wedding I attended. It remains unfinished . . . much like the calendar.

Page after page of 2020 is blank. Void of significant pronouncements. Right up until October 20, which reads, "Dad Broke Hip." Then, "Pop to Rehab." In November, there was one weekend marked with something completely different: a two-day escape with a friend to Merritt Island. Then the day before Thanksgiving, "Dad Discharge." December, again, is blank.

Don't get me wrong. It's not that I did nothing with my days. They were filled with enormous care and loads of love. I have no regrets for the extreme caution we have chosen in order to keep ourselves and those we love safe and well (not to mention those we don't know, but care for just the same). Many of those days were filled with learning and growing, with spiritual deepening, with virtual connectedness, and the acquisition of new tools and new skills in the art of eldercare. We miss our people, but so far . . . though physically distant, we are still all present and accounted for.

But so many are not as lucky as we. Those blank calendar pages remind me of all the lives that were brimming with to-dos and check marks of accomplishment, with no more pages to be flipped. My heart aches for those who have lost loved ones this year, whether to this virus, to disease, despair, or the horrors of brutality. I grieve not only for those who were unable to have the hand of a loved one holding theirs at departure, but for those they have left behind, without the opportunity to be surrounded and held by those who love them, each longing to ease suffering in the smallest but most meaningful way.

I remember feeling so lucky that Dad had remained relatively well all year. I couldn't imagine him being in a hospital or rehab facility should there be COVID-19 restrictions prohibiting visitors. When he broke his femur, I was relieved to know that he could at least have one visitor each day.

My parents and I have stopped doing the whole gift thing for Christmas. So, this year I bought us the boxset of the 90s TV series, *Northern Exposure*. We've been watching two episodes each evening. It is a delightful way to end each day. A gift that keeps on giving.

One of the episodes we watched tonight was an old favorite. I think of it each year around the solstice, as the town gathers to celebrate the rebirth of the Sun, through the indigenous tale of the Raven. The episode takes us through the lives of our beloved community, each unique and fantastic, valued for their individuality and authenticity. Each honors the season of light in their own way, and their community holds space for all of it.

I could weep to remember that this world my parents and I are diving into—with intense longing—is fictional, but frankly, it reminds me of what it means to be Unitarian. I was blessed to grow up, not in a dogmatic religion that excludes the ideas of others, but in a loving community that honors all traditions, and has space at the table for everyone, including Mother Earth herself.

In a year that has made consumerism feel rather foolish, I was struck by a quote from the town DJ and philosopher, Chris Stevens, "Happiness doesn't come from having things, it comes from being a part of things."

Being a part of several, sacred circles this year has delivered great light and joy, in the darkest of times. The big events on the 2020 calendar were few, but commitments to weekly or monthly gatherings on Zoom were consistent and sustaining. We all long to gather again in safe spaces that are free from shields and obstacles, but what I know for sure is that we can do hard things. We can love others enough to keep them safe for a few more months . . . or several, if necessary.

As I hung the new calendar where the old one used to be, I opened it to a blank January. So far, it is marked for Inauguration Day and my fifty-second birthday. These pages hold space for hope. One day, I will get to mark a square with "vaccines" for the three of us. And then, maybe—at some point—my brother and his family will get a few squares. That will be something to celebrate, indeed.

Thank you for walking this path with me. I am grateful for your presence in my life. Please know that if you are walking through your own darkness, or living with the ache of longing due to a loss that cannot be whispered or spoken, you are held gently in the light of love. May the Raven soon carry the light of the Sun to brighten your heart and sky. I love you.

More Eldercare Blessings – March 2021

I wrote about the many tools that have been helpful in caring for my father in October 2019, when his mobility was still possible but greatly challenged. A year later, things changed. Caring for him in this new chapter has brought some additional tools into my parents' home, so it feels as if an update is in order. I am reminded by friends of the importance of sharing what we are learning about, keeping our old people safe and well. May this be of benefit.

One of the challenges for eldercare in the US is understanding Medicare and secondary insurance options and limitations. To bring Pop home from rehab before Thanksgiving, I had to acquire a hospital bed, a Hoyer Lift, and an adjustable bedside table (among other things). Medicare would cover a bed with electric adjustable head and foot, but you would have to manually crank the bed height (a burden when trying to protect the back of the caregiver). You can get a fully electric bed with a monthly fee. And if your loved one has a larger frame (six feet tall and 200 pounds), and a larger bed is needed, the monthly charge is significantly more.

Since my father is prone to bedsores and pressure wounds, I asked for a pneumatic air mattress for prevention. It turns out that Medicare will cover that . . . but only if your loved one already has multiple wounds that won't heal. They care not to prevent them, apparently. Rather than leasing one from the hospital supply company, I found a mattress overlay that electronically moves air through pockets. Thank goodness for online ordering.

Medicare covers a Hoyer Lift for your loved ones who are unable to stand, walk, or transfer. That lift is completely manual . . . but they do not offer a fully electric option, even with a monthly fee. Since I am in my fifties and hope not to require eldercare before my parents are gone, it was necessary to have a fully electric version. This amazing tool allows me to get my father out of bed each day and into his recliner, then back to bed at the end of the day. This gives him some level of normalcy, and I am grateful for this blessing. I found the Folding Take-a-long Powered Patient Lift through the same catalog that provided his recliner lift chair. It can be folded up for transport, but I doubt we'll use that feature. I'm amazed by its maneuverability through tight spaces. We found the U-Sling or the divided leg sling to work best for us. I was grateful to have gotten lessons from the staff at rehab, but Dad and I also spent a morning watching videos on YouTube. It all takes practice, so be patient with yourself.

From the same catalog, I ordered a table for the hospital bed so that we can do breakfast in bed when necessary. He may stay in bed longer on the days the bath aide comes, and she is able to use it for her needs, as well.

We have a Costco membership, so that is where I get gloves and wipes, and doggy pee pads, which protect the mattress, and sometimes the tile floor, where the aim-challenged dogs might tinkle now and then.

Since Pop can't get to the bathroom any longer, I went searching for a urinal solution for someone with dexterity issues, that can serve for multiple uses overnight, when necessary. I found a large capacity urinal with a cup and tube that fed into a larger container online.

Other challenges are related to acquiring the care my father needs without being able to take him anywhere, since he can't stand or transfer into the car. One exciting discovery was shared by his Physical Therapist. I was thrilled with the care he received while Medicare covered home care for a few months after his homecoming, but longed for someone to care for his feet and toenails. They set up a Podiatrist to come to the house, which is when I learned Medicare covers these visits even when one is not receiving home care. Glory, glory! Pop's toes never looked so good! I have no idea if they can be found in other areas, but I suggest inquiring with your local rehab care about services like this and possibly even home dental care. We discovered a place called Tooth Fairy Dental that does dental house calls. Though I have mixed feelings about the initial consultation and recommendation, it was nice to have Pop's teeth cleaned in the comfort of his own bed.

The next big task was finding a new bath aide when Medicare stopped covering home health. This is something they do intermittently, "we see you need help, but if you aren't making progress, we will stop providing that help." I confirmed with his secondary insurance that they would cover a home health aide for bed baths, since he cannot stand to enter the walk-in tub, but when they referred me to the next step, I was denied further assistance. After several hours of telling my story to several people, I cried and gave up. I decided to let go of the need to have that assurance, just so I could get my poor guy a bath. I called several home health services, and found a few that had a three or four hour minimum of care for each visit. Since I am the full-time caregiver for my father, that felt wasteful of a fixed income for two retired social workers, so . . . I kept looking until I found someone who offered a simple rate for bath assistance. She now comes twice a week to give Dad a bed bath, and gets him into his chair—a lovely break for me, though I still found it hard to let go.

The biggest obstacle of the year, of course, has been how to protect my father from potential exposure to COVID-19, and how to get him vaccinated. Gratefully, my lifelong friend is on top of what is happening in community care, and she immediately alerted me to Florida's program to vaccinate homebound residents. A week ago, Saturday, we celebrated the delivery of the Johnson & Johnson (one and done) vaccine to Pop, at home. The staff who administered Dad's vax were also provided with one extra vaccine per household, in case someone else is in need. Since my mother and I had already been vaccinated, I was thrilled they were able to vaccinate an elderly neighbor of ours with the allotted extra dose.

For the last year, my greatest stress in caregiving has been that while handling all of the errands and grocery shopping for my parents, I would be responsible for killing my father by bringing home a virus I couldn't see. I cried several times the day the CDC delivered his vaccine; tears of joy and relief for him, and for me.

When I list out my daily activities in eldercare for friends, that this is quite a lot is often affirmed. While I acknowledge that it certainly is quite a lot, I also understand that we are blessed to have access to the tools we need to make keeping Pop at home possible and somewhat simple.

Thank you in advance, dear Universe, for delivering all we need to keep our people safe and well with grace and ease, and may we be blessings to others, as our lives have been so blessed these many years.

Deep Grief and the Ailing Oak – July 2, 2021

For nearly twenty-five years, I have dwelled within the shade of two oak trees that stand sentinel at the front edges of my yard. Neither are the healthiest of trees; likely accidental volunteers that were permitted to take root and reach for the sky. The one that sits mostly in my neighbor's yard is particularly special to me. Its branches reach nearly across the entire breadth of my house.

It is a squirrel superhighway, leading to the neighboring oak and a diverse bird haven. The branch I spy directly out of my living room window is a perfect perch for our local hawk, and its leaves dance with the grasp of tiny, tufted titmice, who grab seeds from the feeder before returning to a loving embrace. There is so much life happening in and around this beautiful being. I celebrate it daily.

Having recently purchased the house next door, my neighbor has had a number of people over to assist with projects required for a new beginning, and each has mentioned a concern for the wellness of the tree that also stretches limbs over her roof. This is a considerable worry in the land of annual hurricane season. To be honest, this beloved tree has been dropping bits of rotted limbs for many years. The Water Oak, we were told, tends to rot out in the middle, becoming a split risk.

So, I informed her that I would grieve deeply, but that I would offer my blessing for her to do the thing I could not do—tree removal.

Yesterday, grief settled into my core. I started researching sacred ceremony for the loss of a tree. I found a beautiful offering from another WordPress blogger, *Druid's Garden* "Holding Space and Helping Tree Spirits Pass." I stepped into the morning air, and spoke words of adoration to this glorious being, and took photos from every angle. I cannot fathom the emptiness that will be left behind. I cried for our pending parting, for the home and shelter that will be taken from so many creatures, and for the horror of chainsaws approaching to tear into diseased and struggling flesh. The thought of it haunts me.

To come to terms with this inevitable departure, I've been considering how we help our pets to move on, when their bodies are no longer serving their spirits. It is an act of compassion. I have regretted waiting too long, to make that impossible call to the vet. Extra hours of suffering that I might have prevented would be that thing, if I could do one thing differently it would be releasing my selfish hold to allow the arrival of peace.

The most memorable wisdom from studying the end-of-life doula path was Stephen Jenkinson's chilling words about palliative care prolonging death. Much of his book, *Die Wise* was sometimes shocking to me, but I took to heart that I would not choose to prolong death, when that time comes for me. My neighbor and I discussed with the tree expert possible plans for making her house safer, but I realize now that anything other than complete removal would be doing what I would not choose for myself. But still, I grieve. Further, I reflect on the five statements of letting go from Ira Byok's book, *Dying Well*.

This song was playing on Pandora when I entered the house following my tear-filled reverie. *Spiral Dance*, my favorite Australian band, sings about "The Oak" and its many gifts to us, "For shelter and shade has the oak tree grown. The ship, the cradle, the hearth and home. Arms so strong they hold the sky. Stood so long that the heart can't die." My heart is singing a dirge, but the *Druid's Garden* suggests something different—music that eases suffering, and I feel this song will be on my personal playlist. Our playlist; for the tree and me.

I don't know how much time we have left together, but I have started tying cords, ribbons, and bells to branches within my reach. They represent adornments of my gratitude. When the time is right, I will scatter offerings of dried rose petals and white sage at the base of its trunk, sending my love into deep roots, which have kept us safe through many storms. I will scatter stone beads of Morganite, which will bring healing of trauma to the land which will have lost so much.

When I binge watched Marie Condo's series on *Tidying Up*, I was inspired to write a love letter to my home, based on her tradition of greeting a home with gratitude upon entering. I would also offer this gesture to my beloved oak.

> Beloved, sacred, holy being of earth and sky,
>
> Thank you for loving us. Thank you for extending your beautiful branches into my life. You have long stood sentinel near my home, offering shade and shelter for myself and many. Every summer, you host the return of our screaming cicadas and I am transported to childhood with memories of freedom. As years have passed, you

have lost limbs and branches, and I have feared the day when your leaves would drop in the spring, and not return. Yet, you have continued to bloom, thriving through adversity; a body diseased but stubborn.

Every day, you remind me to thrive. You validate my own choice to nurture and support the lives and well-being of others. My own scars, bulges, and flaws are held in the light of love, because I have learned to love myself as I have loved you, even when gravity pulls you downward.

In this moment, I cannot fathom your absence. When you are gone, I will feel empty. Many will become temporarily homeless and afraid. Cicadas will rise from slumber and discover the lack of you. The view from my window will be naked and bright, and my heart will be curtained no longer with branches and leaves, but with sorrow and longing. I hope you will forgive me for being powerless to save you. I forgive you for not being strong enough to ensure your safety. I love you for the roots that have broken concrete, reminding me that Mother Nature is more powerful than anything man can do to limit Her progress. I love you for the trunk and branches of holding, which have been the playground of squirrels that have long entertained the cats who live here. I love you for your leaves of change that remind me that everything is temporary—as old leaves fall away to reveal fresh new growth each February.

Everything is temporary. Everything is temporary. And so, I must also say goodbye. I have to let go. Thank you for loving me and for inviting me to love you back. I will miss you when you are gone every *single* day. But I will also remember you with gratitude and great pleasure, for the memories you have provided. New growth will come again, you have shown me that truth. And just as you have embraced my home and property with your kindness, love, and protection . . . I will be open to receive.

Because of your love, I have no choice but to love again. I love you. Thank you. Hail and Farewell.

Respite to Remembrance – July 17, 2021

Thank you in advance, dear Universe, for allowing words to flow directly through my fingertips, for my mind is filled with grief and fog. There is too much importance to allow for escape. So, please let this page hold space for me and my broken heart.

Just a little test escape . . . a weekend of caregiver respite, desired *for* me by my parents, and required by my body and soul, to enable my ability to continue serving with grace, ease, and joy. Three nights. It will only be three nights. I can trust that everything will be okay for three nights in order to engage in self-care. In order to pour my body into living waters, to be held in the womb of Mother Earth, in order to be reborn. Just three nights, to see how it goes, then possibly plan for longer.

For weeks, I planned and worried. A place to go that will feel healing. A selection of friends who stepped forward to serve *me*. A stand-in caregiver to serve my father at each edge of the day. An extraordinary new neighbor, with an offer of support. It would only be three nights. I had an ominous feeling. My stomach didn't feel quite right. There was a Tower in the reading, and a Four of Swords. Would it be the release and rest I needed, that would transform, or would it be . . . the thing I dare not speak? I worried that maybe we five wouldn't get along. I worried that I should cancel. I worried about the loss of a large sum of nonrefundable investment. I worried that we would get there, then be called home. I worried that something would happen, and I would be hours away. I worried that he would ask me to stay. I worried that he wouldn't ask me to stay, even though he meant it.

There were signs in the days before. Stepping out of my parents' house on June 22, a snake greeted me atop the hedge. Then on July 8, my cats alerted me to a snake on the threshold of my own home that I later discovered upon opening the door, was shedding its skin. I do not fear snakes, and feel that a sighting brings affirmation and reflection. I ask myself, in those rare moments, what might be the message? The assumption: transformation is coming. Soon, that which has become limiting will be released and offer freedom.

The day before departure, Dad wasn't feeling well. There had been a couple of weeks of discomfort. We'd met virtually with the doctor and followed guidance, but he didn't feel good, and I struggled with leaving. I asked him to let me take him to the hospital. They could do tests, and he would have expert care in my absence. I could truly relax. His reply, "No, I'm not ready." Respecting my parents' autonomy as they age has been a boundary I have worked not to cross . . . sometimes stepping on toes. My mom calls me "bossy," sometimes. I have decided to be a servant, for better or worse, and I mean to respect their every wish.

The day before departure, my brand-new, next-door neighbor called me to say that she should meet my parents before I leave, so she could offer assistance while I was away. At some point, in recent months, I had asked the Universe to deliver the right people to enable my respite. I have come to know that my request was filled in abundance. (I hope this will inspire you to start asking for what you need, too.)

I can't remember Friday morning. I believe I stopped by while my Pop was still sleeping. My friends arrived for the long drive north. I texted his caregiver about my concerns, and what to look out for. Don't forget his pills. Drinks with electrolytes in the fridge. (Even though I'm scared, I trust all shall be well.) I texted that night to be sure he got tucked in. The first full day I'd been away since Thanksgiving, when he came home from rehab after breaking his hip—now a virtual paraplegic. Eleven o'clock at night, and all was well.

At 5:30 a.m. on Saturday, my phone lights up with, "Dad Needs You." I didn't know how to program anything else, and instructed him to call me if Mom (who is hearing impaired) couldn't hear him. I would reach out from where I was to deliver assistance. His voice, "Melissa, I'm ready to go to the hospital."

By the time all calls had been made, all five of us were in the living room, four beloved friends holding space for me and my Pop. I called my mom with no answer. I called my house sitter with no answer. I called my new angel neighbor, who followed instructions to find my key and then my parents' key, to open the door for paramedics, who would carry my father to safety. "Don't you dare come home," my parents said. "He is receiving the care he needs. You can rest."

My coffee was served with a shot of Kahlua. I was carried to the sacred spring where my body could receive cold healing. I made calls upon return to the log cabin in the woods. They were running tests. A UTI. Should probably see a Pulmonologist as an outpatient. Fierce daughter reply, "My father is homebound. While in the hospital, doctors come to him. He may not be discharged until we know why he can't breathe." He later threw up, though he'd not eaten all day. My dad told me by phone he didn't feel good, but not to come home. I screamed and cried as my friends held me close. It was the hardest thing to do . . . not to go home.

My Pop was admitted that night. My mom was delivered to and from the hospital by my angel neighbor. More tests. They would care for him to enable my respite. They would call with updates (I had to call every time). It was hard to stay, but impossible to leave. My body, my soul, my heart needed respite. I needed my friends to hold my soul together and feed me the love I had given to others. They, too, are my angels.

We built a fire, and asked the flames to cleanse and purify my sorrow, my fear, my fatigue, and that which was ailing my father. We made wishes with treated pinecones, which burned green and blue. I thanked the Universe in advance for holding my father close, for making him feel safe, and for giving me the strength I needed for whatever would lie ahead. His caregiver visited him in the hospital on my behalf, bringing him his glasses and tablet. He'll want his books and puzzles, after all, while the tests are done and doctors are seen.

On Monday morning, we packed up and drove home. I checked on Mom, then went to the hospital. I told Dad that staying away was so hard. He didn't want to eat. He drank from a cup I prepared for him, but just a bit.

As I type, two mourning doves have perched upon the feeder outside my window. One is preening and looking at me, while the other eats from the feeder, looking up at me, too. I've never seen them do this before, usually gathering bits on the ground. Their symbolism from dying.lovetoknow.com reads:

"The dove's appearance to someone in mourning is often viewed as a visitation from the deceased loved one. The person in mourning senses a message of hope or encouragement from their deceased loved one. Others believe the mourning dove is a messenger sent by angels, spirit guides, or even God."

Seriously . . . they are still there. I see you.

I went back to the hospital to "tuck him in" on Monday night, and returned Tuesday for our "morning ritual." He didn't want to eat. He didn't want to drink. He said, "I just don't know how I'm going to get out of here." I watched him rest. I told him I would come back after a nap. As he did every day, he said, "I'll wait right here."

I was preparing to return to the hospital when the phone rang. The nurse said he was being taken to ICU. His oxygen was in the low eighties. I didn't get to see him. I waited. Visiting hours ended. I called to say, "I'll wait right here."

The doctor said, he had given them permission to intubate and put him on a ventilator to work out the problem. We learned he had severe pneumonia. I told my brother to come. I informed my father's five siblings. I went home to tell my mom.

On Wednesday, my brother and sister-in-law drove up, as my father's only out-of-state brother drove down with his wife. In the rest of the hospital, COVID-19 restrictions meant that a patient could only have two visitors per day. Gratefully, ICU patients could have two visitors at a time.

We sat by his side, watching the machine do its thing. I remembered how it was reported that many COVID-19 patients did not survive coming off of the ventilator. They assured me this wasn't COVID-19, so there was hope.

My parents have gifted my brother and me with preparedness. When they moved closer to me, they updated their will, gave each of us power of attorney, established the line of healthcare advocacy, and advance directive/five wishes. (The male cardinal has just stopped by the feeder for a bite, my symbol for my love language, "showing up." Thank you, love, for showing up today.)

In my father's notes, he declared that his wish was not to prolong death. He listed what he considered to be life-support treatment to include: major surgery, blood transfusion, dialysis, antibiotics, procedures, devices, medications, (other than to keep him pain free) should not be used to prolong life. He wrote, "I have lived my life with love and service to others, made my own mistakes, suffered my own pains. When it is time to leave, I only wish to do so with love and dignity." He marked the box that read: If I am close to death: I do not want life-support treatment. If it has been started, I want it stopped.

I discussed these things with the doctor. We agreed to give it some time while the family gathered. On Thursday, as my brother and I sat with Dad, before he and his wife would return home to care for my sister's mother with Alzheimer's, and their teenage granddaughter, I heard a beautiful voice from a nearby room.

Out stepped a woman with a guitar, and so I inquired. By prescription, patients in ICU could have music therapy. Lexa offered to give therapy in advance and get permission later.

The tufted titmice are now here . . . more than I've seen before. Usually four at a time, but today at least six or eight (the prayers that you are speaking over your life are heard and the tufted titmouse is a reminder that blessings are forthcoming. It is a symbol of faith. And an encouraging message for you to keep it.). And the female cardinal is peering down from the oak branch.

The therapist asked for a favorite song or genre, and I told her that he prefers folk music. She found John Denver, and when I heard the first title, I knew it was right. A lifelong friend of mine used to come to our house for safe haven when we were young, and she had been distressed that dad was so ill while she was traveling for work. The song Lexa performed for Pop was "Sunshine on My Shoulders." I recorded and I cried. She dedicated it not only to Pop, but to my brother and me. As hard as it was for me not to leave respite, I know it was hard for he and his wife to go back home. Seeing how music affected Pop, I set up his tablet to stream the folk music channel on Amazon. I told him I would see him tomorrow, but he didn't say, "I'll wait right here."

On Friday, I felt a shift. I was talking to Dad as I walked about the house, pouring my morning gratitude into coffee. "Thank you in advance, dear angels, for holding my father in the light of love, and for guiding me toward right action." I pulled a card from Alana Fairchild's Journey of Love Oracle, and the message was, *soft*. It was number forty-seven and the message was on page 111. It read as follows:

> A sanctuary bathed in soft light, your heart is receptive, inviting, and gentle. It brings strength to the weary, comfort to the lonely, and healing to the wounded. It is a magnet for all that is needed—for you, your beloveds, your world. Don't imagine you must always be the fighter, going against the part of your nature that longs for harmony and peace. This is your time to be soft. To surrender. To let the subtle waves of the heart invite love in, and to receive. In doing so, you will give so much.
>
> This oracle brings you a message of peace. Surrender now. Be soft. Even just for this moment of quiet reflection. You have perhaps been working too hard at growing and living. Take some moments to replenish and allow the divine to help you, dear one. Be soft so you are receptive to the divine. It is when we let go that we truly perceive the obstacles that lie between us and oneness with the divine lover. Let go and perceive that the divine lover is already awakening in your heart.
>
> *You are the softness he desires*
> *You help light his way*
> *You nurture all*
> *That he holds dear*
> *Though tempest clouds dismay*

And in the quiet of the storm
His gentleness comes through
And in the shelter of his arms
His heart is there for you

When I got to Dad's room, his skin was red with fever, and his heart rate was more than double its norm. They were allowing him to breathe on his own with the ventilator only offering oxygen. This, they said, was the process of trying to take someone off of the ventilator . . . letting them strengthen, then rest, then strengthen some more.

I texted my mother, my brother, and my father's siblings, and I told them that I felt we should let him go. Though it pained us all, we were in agreement. We chose not to betray him. We chose to honor his wishes. We are capable of hard things. This is the hardest thing I have ever done. I spoke to two doctors and his nurses. If we took him off life support, he would not survive. If we kept him on for weeks to see if medication and machines could manufacture a new beginning, we would risk bringing him back to the surface, only to suffer the continued pain of life inside a broken, eighty-four-year-old body. He would eventually be moved out of ICU, and placed where the care would not be "intensive," but lacking.

Daddy's siblings came to see him and to say goodbye. They felt the decision was the right action. Since he is the eldest of seven, they were saying farewell to a brother they had known every single day of their lives. We talked about our history of lost loves, regrets, and signs. My Uncle told me that as he and his wife read my post that morning about the oracle card I had drawn, his wife had opened her wallet to reveal their room key, partially obscured in its pocket, it read, "It's Time to Let Me Go."

Between visitors, I read to my father. On his first day on the ventilator, I read to him poetry by David Whyte and John O'Donahue. And then I read him my latest blog post about the tree in my neighbor's yard that will soon be removed. As I read those words to him, I realized that every word of *Deep Grief and the Ailing Oak,* had been written for him. Seriously. *Every.* Word.

When Mom visited Dad, it was hard. They'd lived together for sixty years, and didn't really talk much when he was not unconscious. She wasn't sure what to say when it seemed he wasn't listening. But I assured her that he could hear us. That night, she sent me a message that read, "You know what Dad likes? Winnie the Pooh." And so, that is how I spent the last full day with my father, reading to him the book that he once read to me. I remember the four of us circled in the living room, taking turns reading chapters as I was learning to read.

After five chapters, I reminded Daddy that when his body was gone from us, he was instructed to haunt us. My brother and I both requested that he show up to us in ways that we could understand. Every morning, when I lifted him out of bed and into his chair, he insisted on listening to his music. With a love of folk music, I found a station and pressed play. Here were the first three songs that played before visiting hours ended, and I was forced to leave him behind, hearing him say, "I'll wait right here." "Sailing" by Christopher Cross, "Just a dream and the wind to carry me, and soon I will be free." Followed by, "Just the Way You Are" by Billy Joel, "I said I love you, that's forever, and this I promise from the heart. I couldn't love you any better. I love you just the way you are," and the last song my father sent to me before they made me leave was, "You Are So Beautiful" by Joe Cocker, "You're everything I hoped for. You're everything I need. You are so wonderful to me."

Okay Pop . . . music it is. You will communicate to me, in part, through music. I'm listening.

That night, I came home and asked our friends and loved ones to hold my father close. I shared the words of the *phowa* practice, and asked them if they would say this prayer, or one of their own, on his behalf. So many responded. We are wealthy in our friends. I asked one friend to drive my mother and me to the hospital the next day, and my lifelong friend flew in to stay the night and say goodbye to the father figure that she deserved. I spoke to the owner of our local crematorium, who I discovered during end-of-life doula studies a few years earlier. We shared deep, meaningful conversation and more than one synchronicity. I decided to commit the sacred vessel of my father to her care, when it was time.

I probably don't have to write down for posterity that it was impossible to sleep, or how a body holding grief and empathy for the dying feels not a single inch of comfort. Everything is clenched from scalp to toes. The grieving become the embodiment of pain and suffering.

On Saturday morning, we moved through thickness and nausea. Not a moment spent without question. Is he ready to go? Are we ready to let go? How will we survive this day? Are we making a mistake? Will he suffer? Is he suffering? Will we collapse under the weight of not knowing? Have I misread the signs? From his advance directive and five wishes, have I betrayed him by waiting this long? Have I betrayed him by not waiting long enough? Will my knees fall out from under me? Have I prepared the right words for his soul to hear? Will he follow them into the light of all that is? Will he be stubborn and choose to remain in suffering, just to be with us for a while longer . . . like that Thursday before my trip, when I asked him to let me take him to the hospital? He is the one on the ventilator, so why am I the one that can't breathe? Daddy—daddy . . . I love you.

We arrived at the hospital and our friends and companions said their goodbyes, and we all stepped out after the paperwork was signed and respiratory therapist came in to remove all of the tubing that filled my father's mouth, throat, and nose. My mother and I returned alone, and I called my brother and sister-in-law, who wanted to be with us, though they could not be physically present.

The nurse would come in to ensure Dad was comfortable. There was a gurgle of moisture in his throat. His eyes were closed, but when we spoke, he would turn his head. Should I have opened his eyes for him? Did I fail him again?

I spoke the words of *phowa*, and asked that he know he was forgiven for anything that he may have thought or done, and that we hoped he would forgive us. When my mother spoke those words, "I forgive you, and I hope you forgive me," he turned his head toward her and his mouth changed shape, though he could not speak. In that gesture, I know there was forgiveness between them.

Dad's brother, who had driven down when he'd heard the news, joined us in the room. He was committed to being present for all of us. I read a poem shared by a friend, written by Byron Ballard. The words are stirring and felt just right. We looked out the window, and the puffy clouds created a blue opening in the sky. I read these words and invited my father to go through the portal, just like in Stargate. It is open and ready for your next adventure.

"A Prayer for the Dead" by H. Byron Ballard, *Earth Works: Ceremonies in Tower Time*

You have come to the end of this pathway in a journey to which we bear witness. You have come to the end of a pathway that is barred with a gate and a door. May this door open swiftly and silently. May this gate give you a moment's grace in which to rest your spirit before you venture through.

We stand here with you, as your companions, as your family, for you are beloved. But, for now, we must remain here. We cannot go with you to this old land. Not yet.

For you will see the Ancestors. You will see the Beloved Dead. You will walk among the Divine Beings that guide and nurture us all. You go to dwell in the lands of summer and of apples, where we dance forever youthful, forever free. We can hear the music in the mist, the drums that echo our sad hearts. We can see your bright eyes and your smile.

And so, we open the gate. We push back the door. We hold the gate open. We glance through the doorway, and with love and grief and wonder . . . we watch you walk through. Hail the Traveler! All those remembered in love, in honor, live on. Farewell, o best loved, o fairest, farewell.

I reread to him the slightly edited letter that I thought I was writing to my ailing oak tree, but found it to be truly for him.

Beloved, sacred, holy being of earth and sky,

Thank you for loving us. Thank you for extending your beautiful presence into our lives. You have long stood sentinel in our lives, offering protection and shelter for us and many. Every morning, you have greeted my return with warm welcome and I am transported to childhood with memories of freedom. As years have passed, you have lost strength and ability, and I have feared the day when your body would sever its commitment to your soul and fail your intention to return. And yet, you have continued to rise, thriving through adversity . . . a body diseased but stubborn.

Every day, you remind me to thrive. You validate my own choice to nurture and support the lives and well-being of others. My own scars, bulges, and flaws are held in the light of love, because I have learned to love myself as I have loved you, even when gravity pulls you downward.

In this moment, we cannot fathom your absence. When you are gone, we will feel empty. Many will become temporarily homeless and afraid.

Friends will reach for your sheltering love and discover the lack of you. The view from our heartbroken souls will be naked and bright, and our hearts will be curtained no longer with your warmth and love, but with sorrow and longing.

I hope you will forgive me for being powerless to save you. I forgive you for not being strong enough to ensure your safety. I love you for the roots that you planted for the good health and future of our family. I love you for the light you offered to allow us to grow, while being ever present as safe harbor for those who call you husband, father, brother and friend. I love you for your example of surrender, that reminds me that everything is temporary—as what is no longer needed gently falls away to reveal fresh new growth.

Everything is temporary. Everything is temporary. And so, we must also say goodbye. We have to let you go. Thank you for loving us and for inviting us to love you back. We will miss you when you are gone every single day. But we will also remember you with gratitude and great pleasure, for the memories you have provided. New growth will come again, you have shown us that truth. And just as you have embraced our lives with your kindness, love and protection . . . we will be open to receive.

Because of your love, we have no choice but to love again. We love you. Thank you. Hail and Farewell.

I chanted the healing chant and the river is flowing chant, that I once sang to my goddess babies in their mothers' bellies. I played a piece of music a member of our beloved church community shared with me that morning. The nurse came in to bring him more comfort. The gurgling was still there, and she left to ask the doctor about giving him another dose of something to dry it. My uncle stepped away for a few moments.

I pushed play on the Amazon folk channel I'd been playing each night when I left him. It had stopped with the question, "are you still listening?" Wondering how long his body would choose to hold onto his tethered soul, I hoped it would bring comfort. And here is what had been waiting to be played all day, "The Air that I Breathe," by the Hollies, to my mother, my brother, to my sister-in-law, and to me . . . my father sent this message, "All I need is the air that I breathe and to love you." We laughed and we cried, for the irony of a beautiful being whose lungs could not hold oxygen. We watched the number growing smaller and smaller, and we were all honored and heartbroken to bear witness to the grand departure of our beloved Traveler as he walked through the gate. It was 1:52 p.m. at his last visible breath, and 2:02 p.m. at his final heartbeat. My new Angel number . . . 202. When I see it, I will know he is near.

"Peace came upon me and it leaves me weak, so sleep silent angel, go to sleep."

Thank you for walking this path with us. There is a long, long way yet to go on this journey of grief, and we know we are not alone.

I love you, Daddy. Send me the songs and the signs, please. I'll wait right here.

The Burden of Light – July 2021

This week has been so heavy. It has been filled with monumental loss. Not unexpected, like the loss of my father just ten days earlier, but horrifyingly painful, nonetheless.

The ailing oak in my neighbor's yard, which has blessed my property with glorious shade, beautiful wildlife, and extraordinary character for decades, was suddenly scheduled to come down.

My angel neighbor, who had been fully present for the care of my parents during my (supposed) respite weekend, felt the stress of it all. She was warned of the insecurity of a tree with wounds that would not heal. There was risk to both of our homes. She was aware of how deeply connected her new neighbor was to the tree for which she had the responsibility to secure.

I knew it would be hard. I struggled with whether I could be fully present for the dismantling. It felt like the honorable thing to do . . . not to let a sacred being pass from the world without holding space and bearing witness. So, I stayed.

I missed the beginning of the work, due to a doctor appointment. I had one request for keeping a section intact, a branch that extended like a fork, where the hawk would perch, and the tufted titmice would gather to fly back and forth to the feeder. I would trim the leaves and create an art installation, so that it would remain in my life, in a new form. When I got home, that sacred limb was already in pieces on the ground.

The tree guy tried to comfort me. There will be more light. You'll be able to grow grass. It is of no comfort to me, though. I don't believe in grass. I find it to be a waste of valuable resources. My tree had been cultivated over decades to block out the light and the crowded lawn of the car lover across the street. Its arms gave me the illusion of being in the middle of a woodland, with dappled daylight. The sun hurts my eyes, and I am struggling not to pull the curtains.

I sobbed uncontrollably the day Her trunk came down. Her branches showed no signs of decay. They were strong, and could have seemingly gone on for years. But the trunk did eventually reveal that deep wound. It was deep, dark, and smelled of rot. It revealed the threat, the risk, the reason for my suffering.

My sweet angel neighbor felt every ounce of my suffering. I didn't mean to make her hurt, too. I kept saying, "this isn't logic, this is love." I had given her my blessing for the removal, but I warned that I would grieve deeply. I was not wrong. I felt with my soul the teeth of the chainsaw chewing my flesh, and the descent of my broken body with each thud of falling wood.

The tree removal crew tore up my yard with machinery and severed limbs. It was a nightmare in every sense of a nature lover's world view. Now that the work is nearly done, there is so much light that it hurts my eyes. It feels hot and unkind. I feel tired and defeated.

But I am also held and loved. Friends came on day one to say farewell to our tree with a bottle of wine. Another friend came on day two to select bits of sacred wood, to later craft into a vessel of holding for my father's cremains. He sat with me for a few hours, as I told stories of my family's history on this land, near this tree. He held space for the loss of my father and the loss of my oak.

He listened as I worked through all of my own hard-earned wisdom. About how history has taught me that the worst things that have ever happened to me have mostly turned out to lead to the best things ever. That if I had not been catapulted out of one space, I wouldn't have been open to receive when something wonderful came along. He understood the struggle of comparison between taking my father off of life support, and taking down a tree before it has fallen in a storm.

And my angel neighbor . . . she got it all, too. She would never have chosen to do something that would cause me pain. She was being responsible to the safety of us both at the beginning of hurricane season. The tree guy seemed unavailable, and then he was suddenly onsite. We both knew it would be hard.

She came over with pizza and vodka the night before. Eighteen days apart in age, with a shared love of campy movies, we sang together every song in *Sgt. Pepper's Lonely Hearts Club Band*. The next morning, she held my hand as I said goodbye. We scattered rose petals for love, white sage for cleansing, and chips of morganite to heal trauma. We burned sage and three kings incense as an offering. We shared our gratitude and asked for forgiveness. I couldn't ask for a better neighbor.

In fact, she is the neighbor I never knew I longed for. She is kindred. She is another soulmate (I have a few). So, after a day of distress and uncontrollable sobbing . . . I walked out to greet her. I hugged her and told her that she is my soulmate, and that we will create something new together. She was already working on a plan, a friendship tree that we would select and plant between our two homes. We will create a path from her front door to mine. I will plant a tree for my father's memory at the center of my yard to block out some of the offending light, and new life will blossom on this holy land. And the soul of our tree will live on in new ways.

I have kept many branches and bits, for I could not completely let go. A large segment of trunk will become an altar, and at the winter solstice or at *Imbolc*, the element of fire will be nourished in memorium. Everything will be okay.

It may seem like melodrama, to display such dismay over the loss of a tree, but I hope you'll see it as an extension of my love. One who loves deeply must also grieve deeply. So much has been lost these last two weeks. Yet, so much has yet to be brought to birth, and I cannot wait to bear witness to what the Universe has in store. Everything will be okay.

Today, there is a great big hole between our two homes. There is a flattened stump where a sacred being once stood. Like photos of my father, there are only scattered logs and sawdust. The absence of them both leaves me with the burden of light. Maybe I should close the curtains, and forget for a moment that they are gone. It feels like too much empty space. It is sometimes hard to breathe. Everything will be okay.

The tears arrive unexpected and unbidden these days. Not long ago, I could not cry, for it seemed I might appear to the Universe to be ungrateful. I was always grateful! And now . . . tears flow freely. *Because* I am grateful. I am grateful to have known such love and to have felt such love so deeply. I am grateful for the shadows these two larger than life beings cast upon my path.

Today, I hate the light. Today, the light is too heavy. Today, bright light illuminates terrible emptiness. I am grieving. I am heartbroken and filled with sorrow. But I am also loved deeply, and held compassionately. I am grateful. I am tired. I am at peace. Everything will be okay.

Thank you for walking this path with me. I love knowing you are here.

The "After" Life—Life After Dad – August 2021

The absence of my father is such an odd reality. For three-and-a-half years, he was my primary focus. He was my purpose. His care, his survival, his wellness, his presence was up to me to preserve. A month and a half into life without him, I no longer go to bed worrying for his comfort and safety. He no longer suffers. He is safe. He will not call in the middle of the night requiring my assistance and care. He will never ask Alexa to "call Melissa" again. My phone will never inform me that "Dad Needs You" again.

I miss him. I'm glad he doesn't need me. I had forgotten what that was like, until I started looking through old photos. There was a time, long ago it seems, when he could not only care for himself, but he also did a great deal to care for others. I'm grateful for the reminder that old photos provide. My Swiss cheese memory invites me to live in the moment, rather than living in the past. I had been so focused on our current reality that I had forgotten about our past . . . his past.

My father was a man of integrity and unconditional care. Aside from our family, he cared about his beloved Unitarian Church community for fifty years, the wellness of his clients throughout thirty years of Vocational Rehabilitation for the State of Florida, for underprivileged youth in The Boy Scouts of America, and for those who beheld his visage and saw the manifestation of Santa Claus. But all of those things had fallen away over recent years.

He let go of his career at sixty-two, when the stress of his job invited an increase in epileptic seizures. He let go of his commissioner role with the Boy Scouts at seventy-seven, when his mobility challenges and a move to be near his daughter made release necessary. He let go of being Santa at eighty-one, when December arrived and he was in the hospital and rehab after a fall. He let go of walking when he was eighty-three, after the fifth fall in a week resulted in a broken hip.

Long before I ever dreamed of becoming his caregiver, when I was still in elementary school, Pop placed an ad on an actual bulletin board in 1701, a local comic book shop, seeking others interested in playing Dungeons & Dragons (it was the late 70s). My father was the Dungeon Master to a number of teenage boys (including my brother and cousin), who would later tell me stories of how the days spent with Pop in his scripted fantasy world were among their favorite childhood memories. He provided a safe space for a group of young people who craved a sense of belonging.

I love that my dad was a geek. I never had to suffer through the annoying noise of a single sporting event. Our adventures included attending Star Trek Conventions (that's what they used to call Comic-con and the like, back in the day). I had a pair of Enterprise dangly earrings and a color glossy eight-by-ten photo of Mr. Spock playing his lyre. We saw Star Wars in the theater, though I can't say if it was opening day (I was only eight, after all). Though, I can recall being really *wowed* by the opening credits, let alone the rest of the film—perhaps my first image of a "strong female lead."

Sometimes, he went along for the ride on things that my mom wanted me to experience. He stayed in the hotel room, after driving two hours from home for my benefit—while Mom and I attended my first concert (I was nine years old). We were there to see Andy Gibb, live in concert. Oh, how I adored Andy. Oh, how I adored my dad.

I wasn't really a "daddy's girl," though it might surprise you. He and I didn't really have much in common while I was growing up. He was always there, and I always knew I was safe and loved . . . but I think he and my brother had more in common, as members of the Central Florida Atari Club at the birth of home computers, while my mother was taking me to concerts and igniting my passion for travel.

As I reflect on the last few years of our lives, I feel enormously grateful for the gift of every little thing that transpired since 2014. My parents bought a house up the street from mine. My father's mobility was in decline. In 2017, I left the corporate world and was later introduced to 72T, the IRS loophole that enabled an early retirement.

In 2018, I was fully present to recognize the signs of the need to step into a more active role in managing the lives of my parents. The prognosis of a friend with cancer led me to the discovery of a path of study for end-of-life doula. Dad started falling down and needing help up. I was able to be there. I was able to acquire the tools we needed to serve his needs. I gradually learned the intimacy and sweetness of washing his hair and helping him dress. I took him to every doctor appointment, every ER visit, every transfer into and out of rehab for recovery from falls and infections.

In 2020, when he broke his hip and found that he could no longer stand or walk (which had long been a struggle), I asked him to let me care for him as he had cared for others throughout his thirty-year career with spinal injury survivors. And in 2021, this July, when I finally had a weekend of respite, he decided he was ready to go to the hospital, saying to me, "I just don't know how I'll get out of here." Well, we all know how he got out of there . . . .

Sometimes, I wonder how I got out of there. How did I find the strength to be everything that my father needed, that my mother needed? Together we walked through this end-of-life journey, and we all accomplished the important tasks required of us. I am at once mystified and comforted by the truth of it all. When I needed strength, Artemis was there to help me pull back my bow of intention. When my father needed support, Persephone arrived as the divine daughter, prepared to make everything right again. "Everything will be okay. I promise."

Last week, I took Mom to lunch with her salon group. These are a remarkable group of women from the church, where my parents have been members since I was two. I seem to recall that they formed during the last Bush Administration, to share fears and frustrations about politics, among other things. Throughout the first year of COVID-19, before the vaccine, they met weekly on Zoom, to discuss current events, politics, and how everyone was surviving life in pandemic. I went along as her driver, but was invited to stay.

They had all been expressive about appreciation for the care I had offered my parents. I was asked if the online studies had prepared me and served me well in caring for Dad. The truth was, the actual caregiving seemed to come naturally. I had never been a parent, and I had never been trained in any form of nursing, but somehow, I acquired the skills I needed in order to keep Dad safe and at-home. Much of it was initially terrifying. I worried about failing him, a lot. But, when I had no idea of how to change a diaper for an adult, or how to get someone into a sling for the Hoyer Lift, Pop and I watched a YouTube video, and set to the task of mastering the art of whatever was at hand.

I do feel, though, that the end-of-life doula studies did serve me well. The required reading alone, helped me shift my perspective of death from something to fear to something to honor. I was consciously walking my father through the end of his days. Each day that I arrived to serve my father, I was fully aware of the honor and privilege I had to do so. That I was financially free to dedicate my time and full attention to his care was a blessing I woke and spoke gratitude for each day. Having the capability and desire to give him the love and compassion everyone deserves at the end of life was a gift to him, to myself, and to my whole family. There were times when the stress of it all was overwhelming, but I was very careful not to wish it away. Not to *wish him* away. But when it was time to let him go, I knew how to respect his wishes and had the strength to do so.

I had trouble finding tears during those difficult days. I suspect my consciousness didn't want the Universe to find me ungrateful. I often found myself aching for his suffering, rather than my own burden. With so many health issues and physical limitations, he was pretty much always uncomfortable. Either from osteoarthritis or neuropathy. It was difficult to witness his suffering without being able to fix it. All I could do was hold space most of the time. But now that he's gone . . . the tears come with grace and ease. I cry daily, even if just for a moment. The release is a relief, and I almost hope it won't stop. It feels good to feel.

His eighty-fourth birthday has come and gone without him. The one-month anniversary of his death arrived unbidden. Just like so many of my friends and loved ones who lost beloveds before me . . . we are facing a whole calendar of "firsts" without him. Meanwhile, we wonder if we will find the files of stories that he started writing for me a decade ago, after he, Mom, and I attended a journaling workshop at church. I told him that I would love for him to write down stories about his life, that I might have when he was gone. Mom reported that he was really into that project, and when he couldn't type anymore, he ordered software to help.

In recent years, I asked him if he knew where I would find those files, and he never had an answer for me. I did have a moment of clarity after he broke his hip (I'd always heard it said that people don't live very long after this particular event), and recorded a couple of hours of him answering my questions and telling stories from long ago. I haven't played them back yet. I'm a little afraid to hear his voice, I guess. I miss his presence too much. I'm not sure what his disembodied voice will feel like inside my broken heart.

I still walk up the street to my parents' house— Mom's house— a few times a day. Mom doesn't require the same level of care that Dad needed, and she's been trying to make me feel like she can do things on her own, so that I can have a little more of a life of my own. But it is hard for both of us to let go. We are still working on developing our new normal. I have noticed that sitting in his vacant chair feels unnatural to me, even though it is better for my neck and back to do so when Mom and I watch a movie. I am still holding space for my Pop.

I have had canvas prints made and they now hang in her living room and mine, to ensure his image remains present, even when his body is not. I talk to him and ask for his support each morning and evening . . . reminding him to show up in ways that I can understand. I speak his name to the wind (Daddy-Daddy), and remind him that he is missed. And sometimes, I feel him nearby.

A month ago, I woke to find that my phone had sent two text messages to two different friends. They were likely messages I had sent, but never went through . . . but the timing and the messages informed me otherwise. The first one sent at 11:08 p.m., was to a friend who had asked how we were doing, and I replied about my gratitude for a little extra care Pop would soon receive. The second message sent at 11:09 p.m. was brief, "I love you more." Without a doubt, my father found a way to communicate, in a way that I could understand, his gratitude for all I had done to care for him, and exactly how he felt about me.

Mom and I are slowly getting to the other side of phone calls and paperwork to ensure Dad's death benefits for her are secured. As we do so, she is moving toward ensuring the same for my brother and me, when she is gone.

But we are being gentle with ourselves. There are days that one task is handled, and then naps are had. Mom reminds me that she could drop dead tomorrow, and I insist that would be very inconvenient . . . and I am pleased each morning to receive a note on messenger that simply reads: "Up." Keep them coming Mom! I'll wait right here.

Full Circle—Journey's End – September 2021

Last week delivered the painful blow of closure. My exploration into the path of an end-of-life doula was sparked by a 2018 conversation with my friend, Brian. He shared the challenging news of his diagnosis and prognosis, which prompted my life altering question that blessed us both.

We lived so far apart but always held each other close. We communicated infrequently. Each of our communications informed me of his failing health. He was prone to positivity, but would often allude to the truth of his situation. I worried that I would not know when he'd reached the end of his path. I lacked a connection to anyone else in his local world. So, when he popped into my mind, I would send a text message to let him know I was still here . . . holding him close and wishing him *well*.

Our last reciprocal communication occurred after the death of my father and his first birthday without him. I sent a note, "Sending love from afar. Hoping you are safe and well. Missing you so much. Love, love, love."

He replied, "Always love hearing from you. I wish I was doing better, but don't seem to be making much progress. My legs have pretty much stopped working, so now I use a walker twenty-four seven which isn't ideal, but I'm not going to let that get me down. Continue to be optimistic. All in all, I know things will get better. I hope you are doing well. I'm certain you are!! ♥♥♥"

I wrote back, "Oh, beloved. I'm sorry for this news of added struggle and body betrayal. I wish I were closer and could offer support. My dad died on July 17. Yesterday was his eighty-fourth

194

birthday and last month was my parents' sixtieth anniversary. I'm so grateful he was mine. He's my new angel. I'll send him over to shower you with blessings. I love you." I sent pictures of my Pop, so that he might recognize him should he show up in his dreams. But in truth, if one can sense the presence of an angel, I wanted him to know that my dad, who knew the reality of body betrayal, would be a safe receptacle for his hopes and fears. Brian promised to keep his eyes open.

My worries about not knowing were put to rest last week, when my phone rang and I heard an unfamiliar voice. My friend's husband spoke his name, and I knew. I knew that he was calling me with bad news about our mutual beloved. I had texted last week and again that morning—without reply. I'm so grateful that he took the time to reach, even in the depths of his grief.

He shared that his husband had been struggling to walk in recent weeks. He required assistance getting to the bathroom. It was obvious that the cancer had wrapped itself around his spine, and wasn't about to let go.

He reminded me that Brian did not thrive in a state where he lacked control, and informed me of his powerful choice. They live in a state that offers Death with Dignity, and this is the path my friend chose for himself. His beloved hoped for more time, but absolutely honored and supported his end-of-life preference to avoid greater suffering.

With his doctor's support, a compassionate end was arranged. In Oregon, one with a terminal diagnosis may be provided a medical prescription for departure. I have offered this compassionate care to the cats I have loved. Instead of a long and languishing, or painful end, my Vet came to the house to bring comfort and release. I cannot imagine why this is not standard practice with humans who suffer with no hope of future wellness. I am grateful that it was possible for my beautiful friend. He lived, and left this world, on his own terms. A peaceful warrior, from brilliant beginning to elegant end.

As we spoke, I was reminded of the duality of emotions with my father's passing. Though he could not speak at the end, he left his wishes in writing. Releasing him from life support was my final act of loving kindness and respect for the man who loved me for all of my days. I did not betray him by holding on. I honored him by letting go. Brian asked his husband of twenty-five years to let him go, and he did not betray him. The doctor was present, and it was a blessing for these two lovers to peacefully part in the physical sense. It's hard to describe the honor of presence during our final transition . . . but there is a gentle coming of peace that arrives with the grief of longing. I hope to be so well loved when I reach my end of days.

My mom's friend posted an article this week about people "taking matters into their own hands" at the end of life, by ceasing to eat or drink. It states that one can go seven to ten days without food or water to accelerate rather than to prolong death. But the truth of the matter is that this is still a painful ending, and it is not necessary.

About twenty years ago, my grandfather (my dad's father) was in his mid-eighties, living with leukemia and macular degeneration. He was ready to go, and asked his doctor what that would look like if he stopped taking the plate full of meds that were keeping him alive. The doctor said if he stopped eating and drinking, he would pass within a week or two.

And so, that's what he set out to do. He discussed it with his wife and adult children, and the appropriate paperwork was established with DNR signage posted throughout the home where he chose to die. Two weeks passed, and my grandfather . . . did not. He received news that a dear lifelong friend of the family died in her sleep. He declared it was not fair. "Why am I still here?" He relented to the suffering and allowed his youngest daughter and caregiver to administer a bit of soup and water. It took that sweet man a month of suffering to pass from this world. It was a month of painful witnessing and space holding by those who loved him, too. It was an atrocity that he was not permitted to part in comfort and peace, on his own terms.

There are more stories of suffering at the end-of-life that I could use to prove this point and argue for a countrywide declaration of a Compassionate End for those with a terminal diagnosis who wish to die with dignity, but I want to return to my position of gratitude. I am grateful that this sacred being, who I adored, who came into my life to play a vital role in preparing me to care for my father, was able to stand at the portal between the worlds and step through the veil without regret.

I have a candle burning for him, just as I did when my father left in July. I wrote the words that came to mind as I held him close. The flame dances in the jar, and he inspires me to write.

It feels as if my world has come full circle. I was able to walk, without fear, beside my father to the edge of the unknown. And now . . . both of these sacred beings have stepped off of my path. I am so grateful for every little thing.

Farewell mighty warrior and treasured friend. Your last name was the same as Dumbledore's phoenix, and I see that you have lit the heavens with your beautiful light. Your transformation from earthly appearance to energetic form renders you no longer limited. Knowing you has been my great joy, and I am forever changed by your friendship and love. Thank you in advance for communicating with me in ways that I can understand. I promise to keep my eyes and mind open to receive.

Seeking Signs at *Samhain* – October 2021

The beauty and mystery of this time of year has always spoken to my soul. Even as a child, when the depth of my understanding was quite shallow. Dressing up in costumes that my mother had sewn was a highlight that cradled the mad delight of walking through the darkness from house to house to receive sweet treats. My mother's handicraft insured that my costumes were unique and fabulous. Morticia Addams was a favorite of which I was sad to outgrow.

It wasn't until I was in my early twenties at the beginning of my spiritual journey that I learned the deeper and much older significance of the holiday. In the US, we call it Halloween, and it is about wearing costumes and greeting neighbors and strangers with the words "trick or treat." Much like many other holidays we celebrate in the US, the rituals are committed without the reverence of ancient meaning.

There is much written about *Samhain*, All Souls' Night, and *Día de los Muertos* and there is plenty to learn from simple internet research, including concerns about cultural appropriation. A part of my seeking has been to find the spiritual path that resonates with me. Though many friends grew up Christian, I grew up Unitarian and was invited to build my spiritual path from the ground up, free from expectation and dogma.

My ancestry is English, Irish, and Scottish, so it may not surprise anyone to learn that what resonates with my soul includes a foundation of earth-based reverence, and a healthy helping of Celtic spirituality with a sprinkling of mysticism.

In Celtic tradition, Samhain (Sow-wen) marks the turning of the Wheel of the Year, when we (in the northern hemisphere) are moving out of the long days of summer and into the darkness of winter. It's my *favorite* time of year! It marks the mid-point between equinox and solstice, as the days are growing shorter. It is also considered the Celtic New Year (the final harvest—marking an ending before the new beginning that comes with the rebirth of the sun at the winter solstice, as the days begin to grow longer again). It is also known as Ancestors' Night.

I've been on this path since 1992, so this is the thirtieth *Samhain* I will celebrate. And yet, it is the first that feels truly sacred and somewhat urgent. When I started writing about death and dying in early 2018, I recognized the blessing of having suffered few losses, compared to many. Most were not unexpected, and were people I've loved, but was not especially close to.

This year is different. This year . . . my father is on the other side of the veil. I have never longed to see, hear, or touch someone more. Less than four months gone, it feels as if a lifetime has already passed. The longing I feel induces pain in my chest and head. It's hard to imagine becoming accustomed to his absence. But, of course I will . . . in time.

Before and after he died this summer, I felt connected. My intuitive-self felt guided and supported. My inner-skeptic was silenced by what resonated as truth and comfort given in moments of longing and reach. Messages came through nature, oracle cards, and synchronicity. But recently, I have been feeling disconnected, and frankly, abandoned.

I went to the mountains for ten days of respite, and though I found deep peace and comfort, I did not find my father there. Though I traveled with my laptop, I did not open it to write. I was disconnected. And when I came home, my landscape had changed. The remaining Oak tree that was a twin to my neighbor's ailing oak, the other half of the squirrel superhighway that used to stretch across my entire yard, had dropped a giant limb. My remaining sacred sentinel is now half the tree it used to be.

It feels as if every larger-than-life, great being in my life has fallen away. My father and these two oak trees have represented symbols of protection in my life. Without their towering presence, I feel unsafe and exposed. It is difficult to navigate a path forward, in such unfamiliar terrain.

All week, my emotions have been floating on the surface of my heart and mind. My emotional support being, now living many hours away, rather than minutes away, held space for my longing and grief, as I shared how absent my father feels. I was missing the messages from nature that I'd come to expect.

Every morning, I brew my pour over coffee with hot water circles of gratitude for the elements, for my guides and angels, for the safety, wellness, and protection of myself and those I love, and finish with, "thanks in advance, Daddy, for revealing your presence to me in ways that I can understand."

The next morning, I reported to my friend, that the mourning doves had returned to the bird feeder, something they started doing after Dad died . . . previously only foraging on the ground. I felt seen and heard. I felt the return of my father's energy. As a skeptical believer, I realize how silly this sounds. And yet, I cannot deny the comfort and joy that returned, simply for their arrival.

The next day, there were three messages in rapid succession that *wowed* me. The first was a sound that my cats heard before me. As I investigated the odd placement of the knocking sound, I discovered through the library window, that a wren was pecking at a mud dauber nest on the windowsill. When I Googled the spiritual meaning, I learned that they symbolize rebirth, immortality, and protection. They are associated with the arts, and those who write. They are harbingers of rebirth.

A bit later, I was drawn into the front yard. It was a gloriously windy day, and the trees were going with the flow—a beautiful dance. I noticed that the uncarved pumpkin on the outdoor altar was oddly leaning. This is where I make offerings to the spirit of nature (a table cut from my neighbor's ailing oak), and my friend's children and I placed a few seasonal gourds out to mark the arrival of October. In Florida, the heat will argue with you about what season it really is, but we like to force the issue, when possible. Upon inspection, it appeared that the pumpkin was losing its youth and elasticity. Since I was there, I peered through the brush to see the tree-sized branch that had fallen from my oak tree, and then followed it around, to check on all it enveloped.

As I turned to peer through the side yard toward the back, I gasped to realize that a hawk was quietly perched upon the gate of my wooden privacy fence. For the longest time, I stood there watching with reverence, as he returned my gaze . . . back toward me, left eye holding me in stillness. The longer I stood, the longer he stayed, and what I heard in my mind was this, "See! I'm right here. I'm not going anywhere. All is as it should be." And the wind shifted, taking this majestic creature, not into the sky, but into the tree by the gate. He was "waiting right there," just as Pop always said when I left his presence, "I'll wait right here!"

I decided to come back into the house, despite the opportunity to stare all day. I Googled the spiritual meaning of hawk, which is: spiritual messenger, clairvoyance, and spiritual awareness. I suppose I will choose to trust the message I heard. Then, nature's winged spirits of air delivered a final, glorious vision.

As I looked up from my second research moment of the day, my breath was taken by an unbelievable sight outside my window. A bird was feeding, whose colors were woven of pure magick; gem tone shades of red, blue, yellow, and green caught my eye. A bird I'd never seen beyond photos arrived with the final message for the day. The painted bunting, according to Google, arrives to encourage us to use our "voice" to speak from the heart, and to add more color and vitality to our lives. So . . . here I am. Speaking from my heart and welcoming more color and vitality.

Synchronicity arrived the next day, when a friend posted a John O'Donohue poem, that spoke to my grief and my colorful guest. As when the painted bunting was spotted, I cried my words of gratitude, "Thanks for showing up, Pop!"

"Beannacht" by John O'Donohue

On the day when the weight deadens on your shoulders and you stumble, may the clay dance to balance you. And when your eyes freeze behind the grey window and the ghost of loss gets into you, may a flock of colours, indigo, red, green and azure blue, come to awaken in you a meadow of delight. When the canvas frays in the currach of thought and a stain of ocean blackens beneath you, may there come across the waters a path of yellow moonlight to bring you safely home. May the nourishment of the earth be yours, may the clarity of light be yours, may the fluency of the ocean be yours, may the protection of the ancestors be yours. And, so may a slow wind work these words of love around you, an invisible cloak to mind your life.

It feels as if, these messengers and messages are arriving to quiet my sense of feeling exposed and abandoned. They remind me that I am protected, and that as the giants of the past each fall away, I am invited to plant and create something new. As I reflect on how significant each of these beings have been in my life, delivering a feeling of being safe, loved, and protected . . . I now find myself wondering what I might leave behind, onto which someone else—fifty years from now, may reflect with gratitude for the loving protection they feel in this sacred space.

Last night, I gathered with a few friends who knew and adored my dad. I bought flowers that he would love, and my friend intuitively brought fried chicken thighs—one of Pop's favorite meals. We watched the 1993 animated film of Ray Bradbury's, *The Halloween Tree*, and reflected on the many cultures and traditions that honor the dead this time of year. And we sweetened our sorrow, with slices of key lime pie, also in Pop's honor.

When everyone had gone, I wrote a letter to my father, and left it beneath his photo with a candle burning as a beacon to call his spirit home. If he came to me in my dreams, my memory did not hold it.

I asked him to continue reaching me and teaching me, to help me release self-doubt and find greater confidence in the messages I seek and receive. He taught me a great deal in life, whether consciously or not. A mindful soul may continue learning and growing from the past. An intentional soul has the opportunity to learn and grow through curiosity and openness, beyond what was previously imagined. Thank you in advance, dear Daddy, for showing me the way.

My final nod to this sacred *Samhain* was a special call with my soul-daughter. She is a medium, and I felt that an annual conversation with Pop might be an interesting tradition to begin. Once again, the skeptical believer is curious and willing to suspend disbelief, until a sense of resonance is found. In the young woman, who could be my daughter—were I able to choose one, I have found deep trust, resonance, and a sense of belief. We hit record at 2:02 p.m., my angel number for Pop. Coincidence? I think not!

For ninety minutes, Pop showed up. What was really interesting, was that he spoke to the many things I'd written about in my two-page letter. His words, delivered through Red Rose Readings were meaningful, healing, and comforting. They affirmed that I am hearing him clearly, and that when I am through with grieving, I may learn to trust myself enough to know that what I am receiving is not just a result of wishful thinking or a creative imagination. I'm mostly there, because I already know mine is not a clever mind, so I often conclude that whatever comes from thought to page is actually coming through me from something beyond my understanding. Affirmed by my frequent wonder at something I've written, as I Google it to make sure it is definitely mine.

A friend of mine told me that she hadn't really felt inclined to seek a conversation with her father after his death. So, I asked myself why I felt such a longing. I was there for my dad for nearly all of his days in the last three years of his life and have few regrets needing closure, so what could I possibly need to know? What I realized is that I wish to continue learning about things that feel impossible and fantastical. Who could possibly be a better teacher than the man who cared for me for all of my days, and trusted me to care for him in his final years? No one. Just Pop. And it turns out that the shift in perspective when we slip through the veil, provides an opportunity to find words for a world of silent thoughts that never found form in life. Life is fascinating, and death . . . well, it is just a part of life. Learning and growing is a never-ending cycle of rebirth.

We are always in the process of becoming. As I gradually let go of who I was—my father's full-time caregiver, I am opening to who I may become. It's all a great mystery, and I am open to receive.

Thank you for walking this path with me. I hope that the messages you seek are coming through loud and clear. I'm so happy you're here.

Messages from Beyond the Veil – December 2021

Nearly twenty years ago, my parents and I attended a journaling workshop at the First Unitarian Church of Orlando (1U). I can't recall exactly what I loved about it, but it involved a binder with tabs and a specific suggestion for how to mindfully access memories in order to write them down.

We shared things we'd written, as we felt comfortable, with the class, and though I cannot recall (read: Swiss cheese memory—

things fall through the holes) exactly what my father read, I can tell you that it had impact. I asked my dad, at the time in his early sixties and recently retired, to consider continuing the journaling project. I told him that I would love to have stories that he would share, even if a little tough to tell, that I could hold onto when he was gone.

I can remember my mom telling me how enthusiastic he was about the project. She said that he was really into it. When he started having issues with neuropathy in his fingers (he typed with two forefingers on a good day), he acquired Dragon Software, so that he could speak his words onto the page. I would often think of that project in recent years, and ask if he could tell me how to find it. He couldn't.

When he was gone, it was foremost on my mind to find the pages he had crafted. When cleaning out his office to turn it into a hospital room, after he broke his hip, I was mindful not to misplace or throw out any CDs that might have contained sacred data.

My brother came home for Thanksgiving. It was the first time we'd been together since he said goodbye to Daddy in the ICU. Mom and I had a few tasks for him, and my personal priority was finding Dad's pages. He had to do some updates, but we were finally able to open and forward three documents to be reviewed. The first one is titled, *Memoirs for Melissa*.

When I started to read the opening of the first document, I glanced at the bottom left of the page to see how few pages were there. There were only six pages in that first of three documents. That's when I knew I couldn't read right through them. I had to savor each paragraph. For once those pages were complete, it felt as if my father's story would also come to an end.

I decided to share one story per day with my loved ones through Facebook. I tag his five siblings, my mother and brother, and one of his cousins who still lives up north. I even initiated a hashtag, my first, as I'm really not a social media conformist. But I did realize how handy it might be to find the series of posts, once they were separated by anything else I may share on my timeline (mostly art that speaks to my soul) on any given day. So, #memoirsformelissa was brought to birth, by and for my father.

When I finished the first document of six pages, I opened the next. Only nine pages, but some of the stories were simply cleaner versions of those in the first document. So, I opened the third and final document my brother and I found on Dad's hard drive. There are twelve pages in that version. It is obviously the same document as the second, but waxes on a bit longer. I'm still not reading ahead, though. I can't. I cannot bear the thought of an ending.

These pages are delivering more magick than one might imagine. My first thought is about the priceless nature of these simple words on paper. My love language is "showing up." I show my love by committing to be present, and by being reliable, trustworthy, patient, and kind. I ask for nothing more in return, and realize that this is not something everyone can offer. When I asked my dad to consider dedicating his journal to his own stories he might leave for his daughter . . . he could have loved the idea, but failed to make the time to bring it to fruition. But that's not what happened. My father showed up for me. He always did. Even months after his body was left behind, his spirit is rising from the pages he blessed long ago. This is my most valuable inheritance.

My next thought on the magick of Pop's pages is the way his words, and mine combined, are inspiring and touching the hearts of others. I've received several private messages from friends who tell me how much they are enjoying Pop's stories. One friend is even inspired to do the same for his daughters, realizing that we are now in our fifties and access to our memories is fleeting. He's not wrong . . . my dad started writing things down in his sixties. When I asked him to tell me stories in his eighties (after he'd broken his hip, and I feared our time might grow short), he could talk for a good hour, but the stories were less cohesive and not quite as full.

I love that people who knew my father, and people who are just now getting to know him through his words and mine shared on Facebook, might just choose to leave behind their own magick to be unveiled by sacred beings who are hungry for their presence, long after they are gone.

I don't really have anyone to whom my stories will have meaning, but I'm glad for my ability to write things down these last few years. My father's stories from childhood are revealing to me the many hardships in his youth that paved the foundation of his becoming. His early childhood illness and disability (with asthma and epilepsy) carved out the future of a compassionate, patient, and kind husband, father, social worker, scout leader, Dungeon Master, and Santa representative. I can almost see each of his stories as the crafting of a single flagstone that is laid onto solid ground, and as my father steps forward, he crafts another and sets it down. Each of these stories, however far they may come from his past into his future, bring the man he was, upfront and center, into the life of his two children.

Speaking of his children, we have not made it into Dad's storytelling, as of yet, and there are so few pages left. I am guessing that my brother and I will have to write the chapters that follow. I suspect our parents see so much of what they wish they'd done differently; they sometimes overlook the many things they did so well. For example, I know that Dad's parents had personal challenges that made things difficult for their children. But those are not the stories that held the mind of my aging father . . . it was the goodness on which he focused. What a gift it is to hold space for every truth, not just the ones that hurt.

There you go again, Dad . . . still teaching me, even when you feel so far away. You just keep showing up! I'm so grateful for every little thing. I love you most.

SAFE PASSAGE

With the recent loss of my father, I've had more space to be present for friends who are sitting with the awareness of body betrayal, coming to terms with physical limitations that arrive with aging, and who may feel called to make peace with the process of "what comes next."

My friend Sandy is in her early eighties. She has three daughters, but none of them live nearby. She has mindfully secured for herself, the last place she will live, in her current incarnation. She now lives in her own apartment within a senior living establishment. She chose this location, because it is within walking distance of City Hall. Aside from pet sitting, her joy happens to be, peaceful protest while standing for social justice. This is how she plans to spend the rest of her time here.

She has also become my first client. She knew my father, and followed our journey with great appreciation. And so, she has chosen to take Persephone's hand for planning her own safe passage. Her mother lived to be ninety-nine, and so we are anticipating a very long, and slow-paced walk forward. She is fearless, but in no rush to get there. Her paperwork is mostly complete, but we will soon discuss the specifics of her preferences for care. If she cannot create the atmosphere for herself, how might we create sacred space on her behalf? She has her advance directive all set, but what music would soothe her soul should she not be able to request it? I've known her since the beginning of my own spiritual journey, so I have an idea of what that might look like, but as I did for my father, I will do my best to honor her every desire, and support her daughters, as we all . . . let go.

Surrender is a word that keeps rising to mind, in conversations. As we age, our bodies begin to remind us that there are things we simply cannot do alone. It seems that current society has sold us a lie . . . that we must carry our own burdens, walking through the world alone, without ever asking for help. But I believe differently. We know that ancient societies were tribal, communal. Once upon a time, families remained connected, as grandparents and grandchildren grew older, while caring for each other. The elders influenced the younger. The youth reminded the elders of their own value. They were reminded that they had purpose and meaning toward the end of their lives, even when it seemed their work was done. Our elder loved ones were not abandoned in nursing homes, but were cared for at home, by those who loved them.

That's not a judgment against current day family situations, just an observation. Something shifted in our values a long time ago. The societal yearning to have more money to buy more things, left little room for having more energy, presence, and time. Living in the modern world is exhausting. I have no doubt, that if things had not fallen into place for me, our story would have looked much different. We would have had to hire someone to care for Pop, or he might have been placed in a nursing home. I recognize the privilege of our situation. I also feel the honor of it. Getting to serve my father at the end of his life was a blessing for all of us.

In a time when our healthcare workers have been faced with a harrowing pandemic, it is clear to me that our society needs an overhaul. Insurance companies and hospital boards and administrative staff are paid enormous sums of money. Mean-while, those who physically care for us and our loved ones are expected to carry our weight, with minimal reward. And then, there are those who have spared them that task. Many end up quitting their jobs to care for a loved one at home, or doing double duty, with a full-time job *and* full-time caregiving.

I want to live in a society where communities come together to ensure the safety and wellness of those around them. Where caregivers are also cared for . . . physically, emotionally, and financially.

The hardest part of caring for my father, was finding ways to keep him safe, so I could care for myself. Easier access to resources and respite care providers would have been a blessing. The places I reached out to, could only offer care in four-hour increments. My parents didn't need that much care, and wouldn't have been comfortable with someone hanging around the house without reason.

I wonder about the symptoms my father had before he finally asked to go to the hospital. What if every homebound patient were assigned a monthly visit for checking vitals and doing bloodwork? We only had access to a home nurse while he was having physical therapy. Physical therapy ended when they decided he wasn't making any progress . . . so did the nursing care and bath assistance.

What if, when we were preparing to leave rehab after he had broken his hip, my inquiry for hospice care at home had not been denied? I asked Dad to understand that my inquiry was not because I felt his time was short, but for the possibility of providing him with better care. They said he looked good, and it didn't appear he would fall into the category of "six months to live." My father died seven months after discharge. If greater home care wouldn't have prolonged his life, what might it have done to enhance mine?

One more thought on surrender . . .

During pandemic lockdown, I discovered a few people on YouTube, who offered entertainment and enlightenment. Each were spiritual and intuitive people who would share what they were shown regarding situations of a political nature, as well as current events. One of my favorites is Cash Peters. I am still excited when I open that platform to find a new video has been uploaded.

For much of last year, his "pictures" were of living political figures . . . being shown metaphoric imagery of a possible future, and interpreting what they might suggest. One day, he offered a very serious and emotional video for his subscribers. It was about his own near-death experience. He almost died in the dental chair, when the oxygen failed to mingle with the nitrous oxide, meant to ease a long procedure.

He went on to describe that journey and later, began to look at the journey of others. He calls them transition pictures and soul crossings. The thing that jumps out at me for each review, is that when we leave the earthly realm, we each have something in common. Before we are able to return to the collective, and merge with the light of all that is, we must let go. What Cash learned for himself and for each crossing to which he has reverently and intuitively witnessed, is that we exit our bodies, and find a way to leave behind that which is of false, human construct. Our bodies are gone, but now, we must also leave behind shame, fear, comparison, self-doubt, regret, judgment, self-loathing, control, and attachment. We are ultimately coming into our true selves, by letting go of all the rest. Expressing ourselves with love, kindness, compassion, and gratitude turns out to be what prepares us to merge with the light of truth (which I see as collective conscious-ness).

I'm not sure if I ever discussed this with my dad, as I was learning it from Cash Peters. But when he was in the ICU on a ventilator, and as my brother and I were speaking to him with the belief that he could still hear us, I gave him instructions. I told him about how Cash describes the journey after one leaves their body. I told him that he might find himself alone in a tunnel of some sort, and that it may feel confusing, at first. I told him of the description of Stephen Hawking's transition pictures, and how he found his feet, and walked toward the light. I reminded him that his body has betrayed him, and that it now seems broken, but that he will find, that if he chooses to do so . . . he will walk. And as he walks forward, he will be able to shed all the things that may have held him back in the mortal realm. And when he arrives at the dome of light, I told him that he should do a swan dive into that golden light, because he is absolutely, worthy of that oneness.

That's the lesson for me, I suppose. We all are worthy of oneness with the light of unconditional love. It seems to me, that the path forward, even before we make that mortal transition, is to choose to let go of all the things that could weigh us down and keep us from reaching the light of our own destinies. And, of course . . . remember the Umbrella Principle. Make a plan, and complete the paperwork. It is the kindest, most generous thing we can do for ourselves and those we love.

At the end of life, we can find peace in the five sacred acts of seeking forgiveness, offering forgiveness, sharing our love, sharing our gratitude, and saying farewell. Why not do the first four things right now? Why not release our attachment to comparison, shame, guilt, self-doubt, and fear, while we still have time to share on this planet, and in this form?

I may never know if my father heard me, at his bedside, his personal Persephone, mindfully guiding him into the Underworld. But, in my heart, I believe that if I could have Cash Peters' gift of insight, I would have cheered wildly, at the glory of my sweet Pop gracefully and joyfully swan diving into the light of all that is.

What has occurred to me, especially over the last year, while serving my parents as old wounds have been healed, is that each of us were wounded by our parents. My father's father was an alcoholic and a workaholic and his mother struggled with debilitating depression. My mother's father was unreasonably critical, while her mother also struggled with depression and I suspect abandonment issues. Mom describes them as backward and uneducated. My parents were none of these things, and yet . . . I was raised by wounded people, and suffered a few wounds, myself.

When I asked myself why I felt led to walk this path with my parents (despite a complete lack of training in eldercare), rather than returning to the working world, the first answer was "Because I can." At some point, further into this journey, I realized that by offering my parents my presence, my attention, my unconditional love, and committed care, I might bring healing to old wounds— theirs and mine.

I could see in consequences of declining abilities, a sort of fear of the future. Nearly everything that once was easy and handled with barely a thought, had become somehow complicated or confusing. When things feel complicated, anxiety rises—and we feel unsafe. As a child, what we need most is for our parents to keep us safe and make us feel loved. It seemed to me, in the role reversal of aging, that I had an opportunity to give the love that heals.

I hoped they would see that they have always been worthy of such love. In turn, allowing me to care for them informed me that they find me competent and worthy of this important task. They have shown me the grace of receiving. And when that time comes for me, I, too, will understand that I am worthy of such care. I will have let go of the things that might have kept me from receiving the love that I have always deserved.

We are gifts to each other, and I am grateful.

BLESSING FOR YOUR JOURNEY

I want to thank you, again, for walking this path with me. I am grateful for the many teachers whose paths crossed mine, from whom I have gained awareness and found resonance. I am also grateful to have known that my writing and experience has resonated with others.

It is my great hope that something within these pages has touched on something deep for you. Perhaps to bring a new level of peace with the process of death and dying. If you've already been someone else's Persephone, I hope you stand proudly in the awareness of what a gift you have been to someone when they needed you most.

The path of the end-of-life doula seems newly paved, but it is simply being unearthed. It had become a forgotten art or unimaginable task. We now face the opportunity to dismantle the walls between life and the unknown, built by fear. What a blessing, to return to honoring the entire cycle of life, which always leads to death. I encourage you to make friends with death, and seek to live more fully.

If the origin of the word doula gives you pause, consider becoming a Priestess of Persephone. Greet the Queen of the Underworld with reverence and without fear, and declare your desire to serve those who are seeking Her welcome. If she reaches forward with that sacred garnet seed, you will know that your initiation is complete.

May you find with grace and ease, that you are able to shed what no longer serves you, and when the day comes that you find yourself in the symbolic tunnel of transformation, you will discover that you are carried by grace, without hesitation, into the light from which we all have come. For you are worthy, and welcome awaits.

Until we meet again, I bid thee, Hail and Farewell!

MEDITATIONS AND SACRED CEREMONIES FOR THE GROUNDED CAREGIVER AND END-OF-LIFE DOULA

Throughout these pages which contain the story of serving my father through his end-of-life, I refer to meditations and rituals that I have written, shared, and facilitated.

I wish to share some of them with you, for the benefit of your own self-care. If you are solitary, you can record yourself reading a meditation, then close your eyes and take the journey. If you are well practiced, you may find that the act of reading is enough to take your mind into sacred space. If you are lucky enough to have a Tribe of your own, I encourage you to follow the full ritual outline to be fully protected and guided through Persephone's Passage and into the Underworld. May you find in that magickal place, that for which your soul hungers.

Journey Into Sacred Space

The purpose of the next few minutes of our time together is to step out of the world where we are responsible to others, and remember that we are especially responsible to ourselves. I've written this as a guided meditation that I would speak to you, but understand that you may still "go within" through reading, even without being able to close your eyes.

Our wellness and self-care are more than the concept of taking care of the body that is our temple . . . it is also a gift that we give to those who love us.

You have likely heard the term coined by Carl Sagan, that we are all "star stuff." The particles that come together to make up this human form are the same as those found in all that surrounds us, including the Universe which may seem beyond our reach. The truth is . . . we *are* the Universe. All we need to do to connect with that larger-than-life energy is to simply go within.

Creative visualization is a tool that allows our minds to release our worries of the future and our regrets of the past. It takes us on a journey that is at once outside of ourselves and deep within. It provides a sort of guidance along a path which our minds may travel, in order to find focus and nurture intention as we create a foundation for the reality that we desire for ourselves. Guided visualization doesn't require that you go where the reader takes you, but that you follow the voice to find the path that you wish to blaze.

Consider that you are being given a metaphor or a story outline into which you have the opportunity to fill in the blanks, or to create your very own tale of becoming.

So now, I invite you to find your comfort, whether seated or reclining. If you choose to lie down, be sure that you are not too close to needing a nap. Though, should you suddenly wake to find you have slept through parts of this journey, know that you have not done anything wrong. Your mind and body will take you exactly where you need to go.

We will begin with deep breaths that make your belly rise. And then we will allow our breath to settle into a normal flow, In through the nose, and out through the nose. If you have sinus congestion, breathing through the mouth is fine, but having your tongue pressed to the roof of your mouth behind your front teeth, while inhaling and exhaling through the nose is recommended.

Our breathing connects our mind and our body in a rhythmic flow which allows us to journey beyond the confines of the room in which we are seated. Being mindful and connecting with gratitude for that which we take for granted can be a simple way to connect with the energy of all that is.

Breathe into your belly the element of air which fills your lungs and delivers oxygen, and exhale with a prayer of thanks for the expansion of your chest as you receive the light of love and release the burden of tension.

Breathe into your belly the element of fire which warms your body and delivers healing where needed, exhaling with gratitude for the inner flame of metabolism and energy that powers your body's machinery.

Breathe into your belly the element of water which washes through your body with cleansing and quenching fluidity, exhale with a prayer of thanks for the blood and saline liquid that delivers life through the body and back into your beautiful heart.

Breathe into your belly the element of earth which creates the foundation for all other elements to flow and grow, exhaling gratitude for the strength of your bones and the whole of your body which holds and nurtures your sacred soul.

We come to nature to be reminded that we are not separate from all of life, we are one with it. We can connect with our breath and imagine sitting on a boulder of granite, warmed by the sun on the edge of a mountaintop, or in our mind's eye see that boulder turn into a billion grains of sand, washed by the vastness of the ocean as our feet sink in and waves rise and fall upon the beach where we stand.

When you think of a place in nature that makes you feel calm and connected, be it ocean's edge, mountain view, or a tree you climbed in childhood, which made you feel safe and held within an embrace you did not yet understand, consider making this place, real or imagined, your meditation safe place. This is where you may go to connect with your breath and enter sacred space.

Sacred space is a sanctuary. It can be any place that allows you to feel safe and loved. It can be a physical place, like a church, a temple, or your living room, and it can be inside your mind, which is so powerful that it can create for you a safe place in which to dwell. The beauty of creative visualization is that you are not limited by physical surroundings. In this realm, you may swim in a pool of starlight and be held in the embrace of the being who has made you feel most loved in this lifetime, regardless of your ability to do so in the physical world.

If you have in mind your sacred space, take yourself there now. Experience in your body all of the sensations that come with feeling safe, feeling free from distraction, feeling present, feeling at ease, feeling loved. Know deep within your bones that this is truth, you are enveloped and protected by the light of love.

From here you are able to connect more deeply with the energetic force that surrounds you and flows through you. Imagine that from where you are, your energy reaches like tendrils of light, downward into the earth and through saline water, through rock, mud, and crust into the molten core coursing with the fire of passion. Gather that source and pull it inside of you, allowing the lava to soothe aching joints as it delivers healing light.

Now, sense the sparkly white light of creation raining down on you from above. Imagine the crown of your skull opening like a funnel to receive this light, which spirals downward through your

220

body to mingle with the light you've pulled from below. This is your connection with your higher self, the wisdom that you have carried with you from a time before memory.

This swirling light of gold and silver moves through your body to deliver comfort and peace that calms a worried heart and allows you to see with clarity your best path forward. Let it expand beyond the boundaries of your body to encapsulate your auric field, which extends a few inches further than your body's full height and wider than your outstretched arms.

This is a sphere of protection that you can invoke at any time with a simple deep breath. When you are here, you can imagine pushing out all thoughts, emotions, and energy fragments that do not belong to you or no longer serve your highest good. You can also command that nothing may enter your sphere of protection other than pure love and healing energy.

Once you have declared this sacred space and the gathering of earth, body, and universal energy . . . sit for a while to feel this love filter through every cell of your being. If you are seeking answers to your own heart's wondering, you may ask here and listen. Feel free to take some time before continuing to meditate or receive answers.

It is time for our journey inward to come to a close, but know that this space is always safe and waiting for you at the close of your eyes and deepening of your breath. When you are feeling frazzled or disconnected, you can come here for renewal and to reconnect.

Picture your energetic being, as if you are outside of yourself, or perhaps looking into the reflection of a mirror. Allow the brightness of the light to fade into the scenery of your sacred space in nature, but know that you shall remain protected and safe.

Now, see the image of your sacred space within your mind begin to fade, bringing you back into the room where you are. Carry with you, into the here and now the awareness of the messages you may have received, and the shield of protection you created for yourself. It will continue to protect you throughout your day. If you begin to feel uncomfortable or out of sorts, you can take yourself through an abbreviated version of this journey to recharge those boundaries.

When you are ready . . . you may open your eyes and resume your day. Thank you for walking this path with me.

Grounding, Expansion and Protection/Chakra Alignment

Close your eyes and find your comfort. With feet planted and spine erect, breathe deeply, filling your belly to expand your brilliance, and exhale releasing connection to mundane thought and worry. Breathe in the light and love of all that is, and exhale to release tension in your neck and shoulders. Breathe in a sense of clarity and connection, and exhale to release any cobwebs of clutter from your mind.

Send the branches of your spirit from the center of your being through your legs, through the floor, through the earth, through ocean deep, through the crust at the center, and into the molten core of Mother Earth. Allow Her sacred healing heat to be drawn up through your energetic extension, rising up like golden lava through core, through crust, through saline living waters, through earth and mud, through floor and feet, rising up into your being, setting your soul aflame with healing light.

From above the sparkly white light of creation falls upon your being like silver glitter, and your crown chakra is wide open to receive ancient wisdom that has always been available at your reach. The sparkly light fills your body from crown to toe, providing strength and protection for the work ahead. As the golden lava of the Earth's core collides with the silver light of creation, they combine and begin to swirl in a clockwise motion. From your internal core, this column of luminescence expands,

222

growing wider and wider, until it encapsulates your physical body and your energetic body and aura with a sphere of silver golden light, like an egg that shields and protects you at just beyond your outstretched arms reach, and above and below crown and toe.

Now, Breathe in the color red, and visualize your root chakra. If it is dull or pale, take a moment to shine it like a crystal ball of deep garnet. When it is clear and brilliant, set it back into place, and set it spinning clockwise within its base. Breathe in this red and exhale this red, pushing it out to the boundaries of your personal aura.

Now, Breathe in the color orange, and visualize your sacral chakra. If it is dull or pale, take a moment to shine it like a crystal ball of deep carnelian. When it is clear and brilliant, set it back into place, and set it spinning clockwise within its base. Breathe in this orange and exhale this orange, pushing it out to the boundaries of your personal aura.

Now, Breathe in the color yellow, and visualize your solar plexus chakra. If it is dull or pale, take a moment to shine it like a crystal ball of bright citrine. When it is clear and brilliant, set it back into place, and set it spinning clockwise within its base. Breathe in this yellow and exhale this yellow, pushing it out to the boundaries of your personal aura.

Now, Breathe in the color green, and visualize your heart chakra. If it is dull or pale, take a moment to shine it like a crystal ball of emerald green. When it is clear and brilliant, set it back into place, and set it spinning clockwise within its base. Breathe in this green and exhale this green, pushing it out to the boundaries of your personal aura.

Now, Breathe in the color blue, and visualize your throat chakra. If it is dull or pale, take a moment to shine it like a crystal ball of dark sapphire. When it is clear and brilliant, set it back into place, and set it spinning clockwise within its base. Breathe in this blue and exhale this blue, pushing it out to the boundaries of your personal aura.

Now, Breathe in the color purple, and visualize your third eye chakra. If it is dull or pale, take a moment to shine it like a crystal ball of rich amethyst. When it is clear and brilliant, set it back into place, and set it spinning clockwise within its base. Breathe in this purple and exhale this purple, pushing it out to the boundaries of your personal aura.

Now, Breathe in the color white, and visualize your crown chakra. If it is dull or pale, take a moment to shine it like a crystal ball of rainbow moonstone. When it is clear and brilliant, set it back into place, and set it spinning clockwise within its base. Breathe in this white and exhale this white, pushing it out to the boundaries of your personal aura.

Finally, with your mind's eye, as if looking into a magickal mirror, take a look at your beautiful being in all of its clear, colorful, brilliant glory. See the physical body, the energetic body, see the golden lava flowing upward, and the silvery glitter spiraling downward, see the expansion of the combined energy of earth and heaven surrounding and protecting your body and being... knowing that you are completely protected from harm.

See the clarity of color and energetic rotation of each of your chakras, and how they radiate and glow to fill your sphere of personal and universal energy with healing rainbow light. From this place of clarity and wholeness, you are ready to offer this light to others. Know that you are a vessel and a tool for this purpose, and that none of your own energy will be given away, it can only be strengthened as Universal and Earth energy flows through you. Only love may enter your protected space. As you go about your daily tasks and especially when you offer healing to those in need, know that you will also be receiving healing energy, and it is not selfish to accept it. Be open to receive, as much as you are open to give. By healing others and by healing the earth, we have no choice but to heal ourselves.

When you are ready, take one final deep breath in, and then let it all the way out . . . and open your eyes.

Meditation on Liminal Space – Clearing and Clarifying

Find your comfort and close your eyes for a brief journey into the truth of your soul. Breathe in the light of truth, and exhale mundane thought. Inhale the warmth of love, and breathe out the tension you are holding in your shoulders and belly. Fill your belly with the breath of life, and push out the purple light of connection to all that is.

Collectively, we feel these nights growing longer and we journey through the darkness seemingly alone. At this time of year, we are symbolically moving through liminal space . . . the caterpillar no more, but not yet the butterfly. The work we do here is solitary and life altering. No one can enter the chrysalis in which we are encased to help us with our becoming, nor can they slice it open to rush our emergence. In the darkness, we have all the time we need to process what has passed and bring focus to what is yet to be.

So, picture this space that holds you as a soft velvet cloak. The inside is lined in the darkest shade of blue-black, while the outside sparkles with starlight. You are wrapped in darkness, but nurtured and protected by the light.

In this sacred space, like when we are contained by Cerridwen's cauldron, we are fluid. See your flowing being swirling into the color red. Let your fears and worries about survival and security rise to the surface of your liquid nature. Acknowledge what you see then scoop them up and push them out of your cloak of transformation.

Now, see the elixir of your becoming swirling into the color orange. Let your thoughts and concerns about your creativity and sexuality rise to the surface of your being. Acknowledge what has risen and then scoop it all up and push it out of your cloak of transformation.

Next, your fluid-self swirls into the color yellow. You allow your false beliefs and confusion about your power and purpose to rise to the surface of your fluidity. Acknowledge what has revealed itself and then scoop it into a ball and toss it out of your cloak of transformation.

Now, picture your liquid essence swirling into the color green. Allow your wounds and fears about loving yourself, loving another, and being loved rise to the surface. Acknowledge the things that no longer serve your heart and scoop them up, then push them out of your sacred space of becoming.

Next, see your fluidity swirling into the color blue. See the blocks to your authenticity and ability to speak your truth floating there. Acknowledge those fears and obstacles, then scoop them up and toss them out.

Now, your fluid-self swirls into the color purple. Allow outdated beliefs and clouded memories and mistrust that block your intuition to surface and release. Then acknowledge each one and scoop them up, press them into a ball, and throw them out of your cloak of new beginnings.

Finally, see your liquid being swirl into the color white. With old wounds, outdated beliefs, and former obstacles acknowledged and released, you are flowing in the purest essence of your becoming. The wisdom of the ancient's swirls and sparkles within. You are one with all that is, without the impurities that once blocked your ability to expand.

The darkness of your inner cloak is beginning to let in some light, and you give your eyes time to adjust. You are deciding in what form and in what timing you will emerge from this safe place into the light of new beginnings. You are setting the date for your rebirth, knowing that you will never again be the same as you were.

You know that when you are ready, you will step forward and drop the cloak to reveal a truer you. This new you is well-grounded in her security and she is a survivor. She is sparkling with sensuality and creativity flows with grace and ease. She is wise and powerful! She is a compassionate healer of self and others. She is authentically walking in her truth. She is one with her intuitive, higher self. And she is creating her glorious future with her connection to nature, and to the light of all that is.

Breathe in this vision of your emerging self, and when you've exhaled the last of that breath, open your eyes to the awakening of your rebirth. It is done, it is done, it is done! Blessed be.

Persephone's Passage –
Ritual to Enter the Underworld to
Meet with Our Lost Loves

Casting the Circle

Starting in the East: attendees speak the names of those they have loved and lost, inviting their presence into the circle.

Calling the East

Into the East we cast our gaze to be witness to the dawning of the light of remembrance. We breathe deeply the clarity of the element of Air, that our loved ones may appear in mind's eye unhindered. With open hearts and with gratitude, we honor the Air. We bid thee hail and welcome.

Calling the South

Into the South we cast our gaze upon ancient embers. Burning from the beginning of time, the element of Fire inspires us to go within and to reach out to those who have gone before. Illumination becomes the beacon that calls our loved ones home. With open hearts and gratitude, we honor the Fire. We bid thee hail and welcome.

Calling the West

Into the West we cast our gaze upon the watery mist. Through floating drops of love and memory we focus upon the veil to witness the arrival of those we love as they step toward us. All fear and regret are washed in the element of Water. All that remains is the purest love. With open hearts and gratitude, we honor the Water. We bid thee hail and welcome.

Calling the North

Into the North we cast our gaze upon the lush green lap of the Mother. Grateful for the strength she gave us to survive great loss, we eagerly await her generous return. Our loved ones have been nurtured in the embrace of the Earth, and we are grateful for her care. With open hearts and feet firmly planted in gratitude, we honor the Earth. We bid thee hail and welcome.

Calling Persephone

We call upon the maiden of flowers and the goddess of the Underworld. Persephone, whose sacrifice to the dead brings a mother's grief and a blanket of cold upon the earth. Persephone, whose great heart and deep love offers the rich red seeds of welcome to all who seek entrance into the world beyond that which the living may see. With reverence we reach to you with hope and gratitude, for the honor of perhaps connecting with those we love once more. We ask to be anointed by your sacred waters of clarity, that our third eye may be fully opened to greet them with the ability to see them and hear them clearly.

Persephone of the Underworld, our hearts are open to receive your blessing. We bid thee hail and welcome.

Attendees are anointed with water or oil upon third eye. For my mountain retreat, I used water from the river near the house in which we gathered. It was significant because when our retreat was ending, we wrote the names of our lost loves upon fall leaves, and offered them back to the symbolic river between the living and dead.

"Let this anointing water be your passage over the River Styx and into the Underworld."

Purpose

Tonight, we gather as the veil between the worlds is at its thinnest. We stand ready to receive our loved ones who are lost to us in body, but ever present to us in their energetic form. We wish to remind them of our love and devotion, and to show them that we have chosen to free ourselves and them from familial DNA patterns and trauma, liberating past, present, and future descendants, and to carry these lost loves with us into the future with reverence, and without regret, with joy and without sorrow.

We know that they left us early to remind us of the importance of living fully now. We are here to make that contract with them, to affirm that their loss *to* us was not lost *on* us. We each have chosen to step to the edge of the Underworld tonight, to take their hands and look into their eyes, to hear their words and receive our commitment.

Meditation Into the Underworld

Close your eyes, take a deep, cleansing breath, and settle in for a journey inward. Our loved ones reside in our hearts, eternally entwined in the cloth of our being . . . this is where we go to meet them when the veil grows thin.

Imagine yourself at the edge of a mountain top, crystalline lake. The sky is dark and filled with stars which reflect and dance upon the water. The air is cool, but the water is warm as you disrobe and step into and lean back into the mirror of the night sky. You are floating in the cloak of the dark goddesses' embrace. You feel completely safe and enveloped in love. As your body glides with grace and ease through the silky water and starlight, you are overcome with the knowledge that you are not separate from the Universe that surrounds you, and you are not just one with it . . . you *are* the Universe made manifest. Where you once felt powerless, you now become powerful.

As you look around, you can see a shimmering light below, and you swim through the magickal waters. As you dive below the surface of silk and stars you find you are able to breathe and glide with ease. Where you once felt the limitations of age within your

230

limbs, you now find strength and grace as the healing water has its way with you, soothing and healing aches and pains.

Joyfully and with anticipation you swim into the field of golden glow you could see from above, to find the mouth of an illuminated cave of moonstone and quartz. Three steps lead you out of the water and into the entrance. One step and warm air greets you and dries your hair and skin. Two steps and your eyes adjust to the crystalline beauty before you. Three steps and your awareness falls upon a robe of your favorite fabric of the richest, most pleasing color.

You dress, and begin to follow the crystal corridor which reflects the light of illumination beyond. Each step reveals new colors and textures within the stone, and you are comforted by the healing energy that resonates through floor and wall. As you round the corner that reveals the source of light, you are met by the radiant flame of two torches.

Between twin flames stands our great lady—Persephone, in her wise and nurturing form, Lady of the Underworld. She wears a robe of purest white with a ribbon of crimson at her throat. She carries an aura of wisdom that assures you of your safety on the path before you. She offers you a blessing as she anoints your third eye with the nectar of pomegranate and honey. She points the way forward, as you continue your journey into the underworld to the sacred meeting place of those you long to see.

Now anointed, a path appears which you could not previously see. You pass through a doorway into a central chamber. There is a soft, comfy couch in the center of the room the color of Persephone's ribbon. A fireplace is lit with a brilliant, warming flame, the crackle and pop carrying you into a reverie of fireside circles and voices mingled in joyful song.

As you look around the room, you see there are gold framed paintings that surround you. You look closely, and realize they are portraits of the loved ones you've lost, as well as your ancestors, whom you have not yet met. Since this is a magickal world, you realize that they can see you . . . they recognize you . . . and in their eyes you can see their pride in you, as their smiles grow brighter.

Now you notice that there is a doorway you had not seen before. It is framed in rose quartz and it is covered by a sheer veil the color of moonlight. You are noticing the shimmer upon this magickal veil, when a face appears on the other side. It is the one you love, whom you've hoped to see. Your loved one gently pulls away the veil, and steps into the room . . . in the flesh, standing before you . . . with open arms. You embrace, and take a seat upon the comfy couch, and share a long overdue conversation that brings you peace. Take the time to say what you have wished to share with your dear one, and to receive what they long to offer you. If your loved one departed unexpectedly, perhaps the conversation of closure is required, when we have the opportunity to say to one another, "Please forgive me. I forgive you. I love you. Thank you." Spend a little time here, and see who else comes through the veil. You may have more than one visitor and multiple messages coming from the other side. Fear nothing, as only love dwells here. Take whatever time you need to visit, reflect, and receive.

Our time at the edge of the veil is limited, and so you must say farewell, for now, to your loved ones. Before stepping through the doorway and crossing back through the veil, your loved one turns and hands you a gift and reminds you that you will meet again . . . in that place where sleep carries you. When you can no longer see your loved one through the veiled doorway, you glance around the room and see that the portraits of your ancestors are all smiling and waving goodbye . . . they know you will be back for a visit before you join them in the crystal cave of memory.

Once again, the torchlight beckons you to follow the path to the mouth of the cave. You carry with you the warmth and memory of words shared and the healing touch of your loved one, and though she no longer stands in wait, Persephone's torches light the way to your exit.

You disrobe and hang your garment upon the hook that waits. Take three easy steps back into the warm and safe water. One step and you hold tighter the symbol of your dear one's love, this symbol will be revealed to you in the mundane world, to remind you they are near. Two steps and love washes over you, leaving your heart full and happy. Three steps and warm silky water envelopes you, as you swim under and then up towards the light of the stars.

You enjoy your glide back to shore, as your mind swims in the memory of being surrounded by the love of your ancestors and loved ones lost.

And as you step onto the soft grass at the water's edge, you smile with the knowledge that they are always with you . . . you don't have to take a journey to a mountain top or a magickal cavern . . . you are cut from the same cloth, made of the same star stuff . . . you are all that they were, and more. You are whole, and filled with the knowledge and wisdom of those who have gone before. Tonight, you stand a little taller, reminded of the ancient standing stones that remain strong through every storm to say, "You are not alone. We are watching over you and will always support you upon every path you choose. We are one."

When you are ready to open your eyes, remember to bring with you the message you received from the other side.

Closing Words

We know that time moves differently in the Underworld, and that though we long to be with our loved ones, we know that now is not that time. Tonight is a moment when time stands still, and here we were blessed to connect between the worlds.

But time will move on and we shall go with it. Much like when we connect in the realm of the living, it feels as if no time has passed

. . . so will be the day when they come to greet us and take us from the temporary realm to the eternal.

Until then, we honor them by choosing to live in joy and happiness. It would be an insult to their sacrifice not to.

Farewell to Persephone

Beloved Persephone, goddess of flowers and bones. Thank you for granting us crossing to the edge of your shimmering veil. Thank you for bearing our beloveds through initiation and into the freedom of limitlessness. We will carry your light within us through the long winter, until your return in the spring brings the bursting of color and fragrance upon the earth. Ever be with us on our spiritual journey. Hail and farewell.

Farewell North

Spirit of Earth, elements of the North, thank you for your gifts of strength and stability, for wisdom and prosperity. Thank you for holding us close through every stage of our becoming. Ever be with us on our spiritual journey. Hail and Farewell.

Farewell West

Spirit of Water, elements of the West, thank you for your gifts of cleansing and emotion, for healing and fluidity. Thank you for washing us clean of fear and regret, nurturing our path forward. Ever be with us on our spiritual journey. Hail and Farewell.

Farewell South

Spirit of Fire, elements of the south, thank you for your gifts of purification and illumination, for direction followed by action. Thank you for lighting the chamber of our connection to those we love, and for keeping the flame alive until we meet again. Ever be with us on our spiritual journey. Hail and farewell.

Farewell East

Spirit of Air, elements of the East, thank you for your gifts of clarity and new beginnings, for awareness and ideation to guide our future footfalls. Thank you for the breath that fills our lungs for singing the songs of our loved ones' memory. Ever be with us on our spiritual journey. Hail and farewell.

Opening the Circle—Closing the Ritual

May the circle be open, but unbroken. May the love of the Goddess be ever in our hearts. Merry meet, merry part, and merry meet again.

Farewell Ritual Upon My Departure

Where: All gather in a peaceful place in nature, where a circle can be made.

Cast Circle

All hold hands, and the person in the East starts the casting by speaking a word that makes them think of me. Then, the person to their left does the same, until everyone has spoken once. Then the one who started the casting announces that it is done.

Call Quarters

Spirit of Air, Beloved Elements of the East, we call upon your luminous essence to bring to our circle your gifts of remembrance and new beginnings. May our heartfelt gratitude for the light bring rise to the sacred sun as we breathe deeply and express our sorrow and joy through your gifts of words and song. Divine breath, we bid thee hail and welcome.

Spirit of Fire, Beloved Elements of the South, we call upon your radiant essence to bring to our circle your gifts of energy and inspiration. May our heartfelt gratitude for the warmth bring rise of the Mother's molten core through the roots of our beings as we dance wildly and express our sorrow and joy through your gifts of spirit and motion. Divine flame, we bid thee hail and welcome.

Spirit of Water, Beloved Elements of the West, we call upon your fluid essence to bring to our circle your gifts of healing and sweet flowing emotion. May our heartfelt gratitude for sentiment bring rise to calm sensation as we wash away our pain and express our sorrow and joy through your gifts of expression and tears. Divine flood, we bid thee hail and welcome.

Spirit of Earth, Beloved Elements of the North, we call upon your solid essence to bring to our circle your gifts of strength and support. May our heartfelt gratitude for the body that sustains us bring rise to the arms of the Goddess to wrap us in Her embrace as we express our sorrow and joy in safety which brings comfort and peace. Divine rock and bone, we bid thee hail and welcome.

Chant: The Earth, the Air, the Fire, the Water—return, return, return, return. The Earth, the Air, the Fire, the Water—return, return, return, return. A-ay, a-ay, a-ay, a-ay, I-oh, I-oh, I-oh, I-oh . . . A-ay, a-ay, a-ay, a-ay, I-oh, I-oh, I-oh, I-oh . . . (repeat)

Goddess

Holy Maiden, Beloved Artemis, Goddess of Forest and Stream, we ask for your presence in our sacred circle, as we send our beloved sister to meet you beyond the veil. Great Warrior Queen, we honor your spirit of courage which long ago pierced the soul of Melissa, when her devotion to you was immediate and fierce. Through you, she found strength, courage and determination to be wholly unto herself. We ask that you stand with your torch burning brightly, to welcome your daughter home. We bid thee hail and welcome!

Chant: Holy Maiden Huntress, Artemis, Artemis . . . Maiden Come to Us (repeat three times).

Holy Maiden, Beloved Persephone, Goddess of flowers and darkness, we ask for your presence in our sacred circle as we send our beloved sister to meet you beyond the veil. Great Queen of the Underworld, we honor your spirit of initiation which touched the heart of Melissa, when your passion to serve those seeking passage became her own. Through you, she found purpose, meaning, and new life through being of service to the dying, and celebrated her own becoming. We ask that you offer her your garnet seeds of pomegranate that she may take her place beside you, and among those she was so honored to serve. We bid thee hail and welcome!

Chant: Maiden bright, sweet joy you bring, Persephone, hear the song we sing. By pomegranate, willow tree . . . Persephone, come to thee (repeat three times).

Purpose

Today, we gather to honor the transition of our daughter, our sister, our friend. Melissa asked you all to gather here today, so that you might be witness to the celebration of her most sacred treasure. Her greatest items of value are filling this sacred space. Do you see it? Look to your left, look to your right, look across from you, and everywhere in between, and if you still can't see Melissa's greatest treasure, she invites you to look within. In all of her life in human form, she never valued anything more than your love and presence in her life. You should know that she is with us now, in her original energetic form, no longer limited by the body that so graciously carried her soul these many years, and she delights in having us all together in one sacred space. If you close your eyes, you might feel her warmth on your back, or her breath on your cheek. She assures you that there is nothing to fear, and no reason to weep, for she will always be within your heart's reach.

Community Sharing

Melissa's Treasure is invited to share stories, poetry, and song.

When finished, each jewel receives a blank card and pen to hold onto.

Meditation

Close your eyes, and find your comfort. Breathe deeply of the love that surrounds you. Inhale the light of love, and exhale deep peace. Send your energetic roots through your body and into the earth—through grass and sand, dirt and clay, through saline ocean, through protective crust, and plunge into the healing molten core of Mother. Feel her healing balm rise through you, bringing strength and stability to your very center. Now, from high above your crown, draw in the sparkly white light of creation, from the seventh plane, through energetic realms, and higher self, through your open crown, and into your sacred vessel. Allow this light to filter through every cell of your body, making it come alive with effervescence, as it spirals downward to mingle with the molten energy of Mother Earth.

As this energy combines and expands, you are met with a sense of delightful awakening. From this place, you are gifted with clarity beyond imagining. Let me show you, from this sacred place, the brilliant beauty of your body and soul. As I journey from this earthly realm, and back into energetic form—allow me to carry with me your worries and woes, so that you might be free from suffering until we meet again beyond all we currently may see. As you lift this burden from your heart, your soul, and your mind . . . place it into my waiting arms, and allow me to bear it as I go. And if you are willing to receive it, I ask that you lean in to accept a sacred gift from me to you. Allow me to place this seed of loving light into your heart, so that it may continue to grow fuller and brighter with each passing year . . . as you love yourself even more than ever before, as a favor to me in my inability to further nurture your perfection and light in human form. Know that you are never alone, for we are all one . . . forever and always.

Should you happen to see a fluffy bumble butt in the future, know that I have sent you a reminder of my eternal adoration for your dearest heart. I am so grateful for my greatest treasure . . . the gift of your presence and friendship in my life. What a magickal life this has been. I wouldn't change a thing. Now, give me a hug and when you are ready, you may open your eyes.

Ritual

Melissa's treasure each write onto the cards provided the words of worry or burden to be carried away, and then place them into the flames to be carried by Her breath into the great mystery of transmutation, healing, and peace.

Closing

Farewell to Goddesses

Courageous and Compassionate Ladies of our hearts, Artemis and Persephone, we thank you for your presence in our sacred circle, and for your bright welcome to our sister Melissa, as she enters the comfort of your embrace. Ever be with us on our spiritual journeys. We bid thee hail and farewell.

Farewell to Elements

Let the gentle breeze of the element of air be her breath upon our cheek, as she leans in for a hug. Let the warmth of the sun be the healing balm of her presence against our skin. Let the gentle rain be her tears of joy, as she celebrates our moments of joy and triumph. Let the bursting of new life each spring be our reminder that she is always near, in the renewal of all things living. We bid the great elements of air, fire, water, and earth that surround us and flow within us, hail and farewell.

Circle Opening

Chant: May the circle be open, but unbroken. May the love of the goddess be ever in our hearts. Merry meet and merry part, and merry meet again. Blessed be!

ELDERCARE AND END-OF-LIFE RESOURCES

The books that are mentioned in Persephone's Passage, from which I learned a great deal about death and dying were among the reading assignment from Deanna Cochran's home study course, along with others I was drawn to. They are:

Ira Byock's *Dying Well*
Stephen Jenkinson's *Die Wise*
Sogyal Rinpoche's *Tibetan Book of Living and Dying*
Starhawk's *Pagan Book of Living and Dying*
John O'Donohue's *To Bless the Space Between Us*
Dr. Jean Shinoda Bolen's *Goddesses in Everywoman*
Tosha Silver's *Outrageous Openness*

CaringBridge.com is an online resource designed to centralize news and care requirements for individuals experiencing health challenges. It is a great way to stay connected without the energy required to answer multiple calls and text messages. Here, one can cultivate a page that keeps loved ones updated and receive encouragement. There is a calendar for support that can be used as a centralized sign-up sheet for loving care. It is very user-friendly.

The resource catalog that was most helpful in setting up home care for my father can be found at *Spinlife.com*. Anything else we needed, mentioned in Eldercare Blessings, was found on Amazon.com. The compact and user-friendly lift that can be wheeled over to a fallen loved one to help them off the floor can be found at *Indeelift.com*.

Never underestimate the power of YouTube to learn more about whatever challenges you face. Consider watching an instructional video with your loved one, so that you both know what to expect and how to help each other. This is how my father and I improved our adult-diaper and mechanical lift game. Difficult tasks are made easier through surrender, education, and a little laughter.

To create your own end-of-life plan, you can go to FiveWishes.org to learn more and download the form. On their site, there is guidance for confirming the states in the US that accept *Five Wishes* as a legally binding document.

I did not write about what I learned about caring for the body after death. I wanted to mention it here, because I have seen so many pleas for help to cover funeral costs when a loved one dies unexpectedly. Our family preference is to have our bodies cremated. Years before my father died, my parents and I attended a learning session with a representative of The National Cremation Society. Like The Neptune Society, they offer a prepaid plan that frees family members from that worry when their loved one dies. There is a toll-free number to call, and all is handled with reverence and grace. Several of my friends were grateful their parents had it.

My mom insisted we check around before committing to that cost, and we found Amaryllis Cremation, a local crematorium that met our needs at less than half the cost of the prepaid plan. They took care of my father's body when he was gone. Since my name is on my parents' bank account and credit cards, we knew that this would be a simple solution for our situation.

From my friend Fran, I learned about Science Care, which served her husband when he died. He donated his body to science. They used what was helpful and cremated the rest. Her husband's cremains were retuned to her at no cost.

242

Doing this research long before you find yourself in the midst of deep grief is highly recommended. I spoke with Sarah at Amaryllis years before we required her service, and she was a comfort to me when I reached out on Dad's last day.

ACKNOWLEDGMENTS AND GRATITUDE

First and foremost, I am grateful to my mother, Sandi Baker. She delivered every tool I needed to ease this difficult time in our lives. She supported me in numerous ways while I was supporting my father. When she witnessed our struggle, she Googled an answer, and it was on the doorstep by morning.

If there is another book to be published someday, it will surely have been inspired by the healing journey of a mother and daughter. Many of my passions in life were discovered through the introduction and prodding of my mom. Dad has left us to forge our path forward, and this time it belongs to Sandi. I am grateful for it.

I am grateful to start a new chapter and continue my own sacred journey with the loving support of those who will always carry the heart and soul of my father in their very DNA. Of course, that would be my brother, John, and our father's five siblings who have survived the losses of their eldest sister and eldest brother. They are Richard, Kenneth, Patricia, John (whom we call Mike), and Marianne. They tell me that they loved me first and I reply that they had an unfair advantage. What I know for sure is that Billy loved all of us first, and we are so lucky that we get to keep loving each other in his absence.

I have had many teachers throughout my spiritual journey that began at age twenty-three. I wish to acknowledge them all, and hope that no one falls through the holes of memory. If so, I ask forgiveness in advance. Every soul I've met has contributed greatly to the beauty in my life. I thank you all.

Margot Adler, Suzanne LaCour, and Ken Windwalker were the midwives to my birth upon this beautiful way, through an introduction to a Pagan path. It was my mother who found them to feed my curiosity, then set me free to learn and grow. Thanks, Mom!

A huge part of my becoming was nurtured by lifelong friends and my goddess group, Tawanda's Tribe. Those formative years with my tribe were packed with mutual inquiry and exploration, and the contributions of each individual helped me become who I am. With them, I learned about devotion to the divine feminine in her many guises, the power of speaking one's truth, learning to be unattached to outcome, the importance of belonging, and the life-altering power of ritual and sacred ceremony for healing, receiving, and letting go.

There were more recent teachers on my evolving spiritual path.

The one that was most instrumental in my ability to mindfully walk with my father these past few years was Deanna Cochran. Her End-of-Life Doula home course taught me the importance of making friends with death. Her coursework, her school, and her own book *Accompanying the Dying*, offer a wealth of information, not just for doulas, but for all of us—as every one of us will eventually face the end of life with loved ones and ourselves. You can find these great teachings at certifiedcaredoula.com.

Right before the pandemic began, I was taking a course on Holding Space with Heather Plett. She and her course gave language to many things that come naturally to me. Learning how to hold space for a group on Zoom may have saved my sanity throughout this pandemic. What I learned from Heather led to the launch of two weekly virtual gatherings with fellow "Space Holders" and my Sacred Gardeners, who are dear ones who attended my workshops until the world shutdown. These two groups, especially, held space for me throughout the very difficult days of my dad's decline, and I am forever indebted to their great care. You can learn more about Holding Space and Heather at heatherplett.com.

The mystic part of my spiritual journey came many years after the Pagan path began. Amy Brock, an intuitive life coach, turned this skeptic into a skeptical believer. She introduced me to my guides and angels. I see them as energetic beings invisible to the eye, but now trusted through guidance received in ways that I can understand. They speak to me through nature, synchronicities, and my own inner voice. You can find Amy at theamybrock.com.

Amy introduced me to my soul-daughter, Jillian Amann, who has deepened that journey, and helped me enormously through the years beyond the corporate world. She encouraged me to feel safe within the unknown, and ultimately, delivered my father's wisdom from beyond the veil. She is a compassionate comforter, whose story of loss delivered her own new beginning as a Psychic Medium at a very young age. You can find Jilly at redrosereadings.com.

Michelle Orwick taught me about ThetaHealing. She helped deepen my connection and understanding of the power of visualization and intention for healing and expansion. Her words and lessons may be recognized in these pages, especially where they bring grounding and a bit of sparkle. You can learn more about Michelle at magicalmichelle.com.

I learned a great deal about the simple beauty of transition at the time of death through Cash Peters' Soul Crossings channel on YouTube. The perspective he shares is enlightening and delivers great comfort.

I have a huge collection of oracle cards, but those I go to when I need healing comfort are those written by Alana Fairchild. The wisdom and unconditional love that moves through her is often all I need to take another step forward.

Healing exploration was also inspired by Dakota Earth Cloud, a Shamanic guide who we discovered on Insight Timer.

The words of Byron Ballard that were offered during my father's transition were shared with me by a friend via text message. A Prayer for the Dead was written in 2020 to honor those who have died from COVID-19. Thank you, Helen, for that gift.

"I am wealthy in my friends." - Shakespeare and Baker

Six friends offered recovery space throughout my journey, and may not know how grand a gesture of offering a caring place for respite is to the exhausted caregiver. Thank you to Nancy and Keith Miller, Dennis Balenger and Jim Johnson, Helen Hafner, and Helen Schmid. I found deep peace in your good care. Thank you.

Four friends, among many other feats of friendship, were kind enough to hold space for me on a weekend of respite one week before my father died. They volunteered to come along and create a space dedicated to *my* healing, and they wound up holding me together when being away felt important but impossible. Kim Bosco, Carolyn Perrine, Marna Rasmussen, and Deanne Rothenberg, I love you most, forever and always.

Marna was also my father's at-home healer, delivering care for his comfort through acupuncture, massage, and energetic healing. Her care was invaluable to The Baker Family. She and my lifelong friend, Angel Padrigone, helped me prepare Pop's room for homecoming after he broke his hip, and both held my hands through his final day. They reminded me that I am never alone, for we are all one.

Deanne was Pop's hairstylist in his final years. She always left him looking a bit sharper and a lot happier. Being homebound has its perks when your daughter has a loving and talented best friend.

Marna and Deanne were my primary people throughout this journey. They were the "boots on the ground" girlfriends that I needed and everyone deserves. They are my candles in the dark.

Carolyn, a fiercely protective goddess in my life, provided the guidance and support we needed to find access to the COVID-19 vaccine early in its availability, including the ability to have my homebound father inoculated. Alleviating the fear that I carried about potentially bringing the virus home to my parents was no small thing. We are so lucky that she loves us.

Kim is also known as "my favorite tomboy", and was instrumental in the manifestation of the workshops and retreat created for my Sacred Gardeners in 2019. My lifelong friend has been with me from the beginning and will be with me when I die—because I am going first. I love you, little birdy.

Jules Keeley is my angel-neighbor who came to my family's rescue on one of our most difficult days. We are eternally indebted to her good care, and we are so lucky that she chose us to be her neighbors.

Mike McCleskey, Joe Loughman, Marcy Santoyo, Clay Conti, and Mike Priest all held space for me and my *Ailing Oak*. Mike McCleskey is crafting a vessel from that oak tree to hold my father's ashes. These people! I am so lucky they are mine.

So many friends have read my blog and followed my journey with my father. Their words of encouragement and acknowledgement have made me feel seen, heard, and held despite the sense of isolation one feels as a solitary caregiver. Know that you carried me when I could barely stand.

Our beloved community at 1U, The First Unitarian Church of Orlando, held all of us close throughout this journey. My parents joined this congregation 50 years ago, and it has been a blessing that has never failed these grateful Bakers. It was written in Pop's *Five Wishes* document that his memorial service should be held in the 1U sanctuary. If Covid allows, we hope to celebrate the life of Bill Baker at his eighty-fifth birthday this August.

I am especially grateful for those who reached out to share their own stories of death and dying, lost loves, and the weight of parental care. I believe the greatest gift of storytelling is found in reciprocity. Thank you, Kathy Foubister, Janet McNaught, Fran Martin, Pattie Vickers, Sandy Cawthern, Jim Johnson, JT Taylor, Suzanne LaCour, and my sweet Auntie M. Your stories are treasured and sacred. Through you, I have learned so much.

I asked two Pagans and an atheist to read this book and offer brutally honest feedback. Gratefully, there is only love between us with no brutality at all. I'm so lucky they are mine.

H.B. (Sonny) Gardner gifted me more than one beautiful painting before he moved to Japan. A portion of one, an interpretation of a dream he once had, graces the cover of this book. Like Demeter and Persephone, my soul brother and I are separated by a great distance, but we are ever in each other's hearts. I love that the world will see his beautiful dream.

Thuan Nguyen took a portion of our mutual friend's artwork and skillfully crafted the captivating cover of *Persephone's Passage*. He has shown up for me in a multitude of ways these many years, and I love the blessing of his presence on this project. He designed the wrapper that gently holds my father's love story. You can find Thuan at HouseofThuan.com.

My photo on the About the Author's page was taken in 2015 by Linda Baumann. She was a friend and co-worker who crossed the veil early last year. When I see this image, I instantly connect with the sacred being who is behind the lens. Her vision captured the light. Linda's memory is a blessing.

Kaitie Palm edited *Persephone's Passage*. Bless her beautiful heart, she rescued you from the burden of my love of commas and ellipses. It was clear that I have a problem, and she never made me feel judged or unworthy of her good care. I am grateful.

Finally, I found Sharon Lund at Sacred Life Publishers through Deanna Cochran, and instantly felt a sense of resonance. Her area code is one of my Angel numbers, and she has turned out to be the angel who helped bring this book to birth. She is a book doula of the highest order. She held the journey with my father with reverence and respect, and sat with me through self-doubt to bring Persephone back from the Underworld. Without her willingness to step onto my path with her Sacred Life torch, I might still be wandering alone in the dark. She was everything I needed. I know Pop is proud!

Welcome to the Light, Persephone's Passage! I'm so glad you are here.

ABOUT THE AUTHOR

Melissa Baker

Melissa Baker is a Pagan mystic, skeptical believer, mindful explorer, tribe mother, art lover, devoted daughter, sister, and friend. She is a Priestess of Persephone and Artemis, divine torchbearers who show the way. She reflects the beauty she sees in others, and sees all beings as sacred.

Melissa lives in Winter Park, Florida where she cares for her mother and two cats. She finds her bliss through composing and facilitating sacred ceremonies for beloved community, and writes an essay style blog which you are invited to follow at beethelight.blog. The first of her recorded meditations, *Release the Warrior Within* can be found on multiple platforms.

CPSIA information can be obtained
at www.ICGtesting.com
Printed in the USA
BVHW050514040522
635995BV00039B/1662